Delia Smith's

SUMMER COLLECTION

Delia Smith's
SUMMER COLLECTION

Photographs by Peter Knab

This is a companion book to the PBS television series Great Food
Presented by WNET 13, New York
Sponsored by

Produced by

●●●● west 175
productions

First published 1993 by BBC Books,
an imprint of BBC Worldwide Publishing
BBC Worldwide Publishing
80 Wood Lane, London W12 0TT
© Delia Smith 1993
The moral right of the author of this work has been asserted.

Designed by Elaine Partington
with Sara Kidd
Photographs by Peter Knab
Food preparation by Catherine Calland and special thanks to Mary Cox for recipe testing
Illustrations by Vicky Emptage

DK

A Dorling Kindersley Book
www.dk.com

Publisher: Sean Moore
Editor: Barbara Minton
Art director: Dirk Kaufman
Designer: Gus Yoo
Production director: Sara Gordon

First Dorling Kindersley Edition, 2000
Published in the United States by Dorling Kindersley Publishing, Inc.
95 Madison Avenue
New York, New York 10016

ISBN 0-7894-6808-5

Printed and bound in Great Britain by Butler and Tanner Ltd, Frome, Somerset
Color origination by Radstock Reproduction Ltd, Midsomer Norton
Jacket printed by Lawrence Allen Ltd, Weston-super-Mare

Debbie—this one *has* to be for you.

CONTENTS

◇

ACKNOWLEDGMENTS

I would very much like to thank the following people who have worked on the American edition. Peter Mayer for having the courage to go for it. Robert Dreesen for his patience, which stretched across the Atlantic. Sarah Frank and Andy Olesker for the loan of their New York kitchen, and so much more. Joe Kennedy for all his liaising. Jane Garmey for her Americanization. Jane Houghton, my assistant. Mary Cox for her help with testing and editing. Lulu Grimes and Tamsin Burnett-Hall for testing all the recipes in New York. To all of them my sincere thanks.

INTRODUCTION

Is it possible? A really good cookbook from England for Americans? From an English cook? I can imagine the furrowed brows, almost hear the puzzled sighs. Shakespeare, yes, but cookbooks?

It's okay. I know what I'm up against, but here I am, nonetheless, cheerfully introducing myself to you with lively optimism. Why? Because when it comes down to basics, a good recipe is the same the world over. We might have to tweak ingredients, fine-tune the measurements, but if the instructions are clear and simple to follow, if the recipe works, and, above all, if the dish tastes good, everyone will love it.

Now is an exciting time to be involved in cooking, which is undergoing unique changes. You can walk into American supermarkets and literally shop around the world; ingredients are winging their way from one side of the globe to the other in a matter of hours — fresh. This means we can experiment, be innovative, and move into a whole new era of what is quickly becoming global cuisine without boundaries — all this without losing the traditions of classical cooking.

My philosophy during the last twenty-one years of writing recipes and cooking on TV has not suddenly changed because I've crossed the Atlantic. People lead busy, pressured lives everywhere, but at the same time they want to cook and eat well without spending hours in the kitchen. My role has been to help them achieve that by anticipating and removing the hassle, keeping things simple, and, above all, encouraging those with little or no experience to have confidence and to know that they can trust a recipe, having spent money, time, and effort on it.

Finally, I feel quite at home in America. For years, I have studied your best cookbooks and food magazines and have often been inspired by your greatest chefs. For this reason, I'm sure you will feel at home with my book and get as much enjoyment from my recipes as I have had in devising and preparing them.

With warm greetings,

Delia Smith
1995

CHAPTER ONE

SOUPS, FIRST COURSES,
and
LIGHT LUNCH
DISHES

———— ◊ ————

Everything in this chapter is suitable in small portions as a first course, or for a light summer's lunch in larger portions — and that includes the soups. I have included several recipes for chilled soups, as there's nothing more refreshing on a warm day as, say, a gazpacho, which I always think of as salad soup, a way of sipping and savoring all the fragrance of a salad. But for those who are not partial to the pleasures of chilled soups, let me say that all the soups in this chapter also taste good served hot.

If you're looking for a light vegetarian lunch, may I draw your attention to the Fried Halloumi Cheese with Lime and Caper Vinaigrette, which is every bit as delicious as it looks in the photograph on page 9, and the Piedmont Roasted Peppers (page 4), which are so good that nobody can ever believe they are so simple to make. One final thought: As a change from butter, how about putting a bowl of Provençale Tapenade (page 11) on the table to spread on a selection of breads to nibble before the main part of a meal arrives?

————

Chilled Fennel Gazpacho

.

SERVES 4

I'*ve always loved gazpacho and never fail to order it when I*'*m in Spain or Portugal: it really is one of the nicest first courses when the weather is warm. This version is the same but different — the same refreshing, salady texture but quite a different flavor. This can be served warm if the weather*'*s chilly, but if you are serving it cold, do make sure that it*'*s really cold. Chill the bowls first, and add some ice cubes just before serving.*

1½ lbs. ripe, red tomatoes	1 tablespoon balsamic vinegar
1 largish fennel bulb	1 tablespoon fresh lemon juice
1 rounded teaspoon coarse salt	¾ teaspoon chopped fresh oregano
¾ teaspoon coriander seeds	1 teaspoon tomato paste
½ teaspoon mixed colored peppercorns	
1 tablespoon extra-virgin olive oil	
1 small onion, chopped	**TO GARNISH:**
1 large clove garlic, crushed	Olive Croutons (page 7)

First, skin the tomatoes. Pour boiling water over them and leave them for exactly 1 minute before draining them and slipping off the skins (protect your hands with a cloth if the tomatoes are too hot). Then chop the tomatoes roughly.

Next, trim the green fronds from the fennel (reserve these for a garnish) and cut the bulb into quarters. Trim away a little of the central stem at the base and slice the fennel into thinnish slices. Now place these in a saucepan with a little salt and measure in 2 cups of water. Bring to a simmer, cover, and simmer gently for 10 minutes.

Meanwhile, crush the coriander seeds and peppercorns in a mortar and pestle. Then heat the oil in a large saucepan and add the crushed spices, along with the chopped onion. Let these cook gently for 5 minutes, then add the crushed garlic and cook for a further 2 minutes. Now add the balsamic vinegar, lemon juice, chopped tomatoes, and oregano. Stir well, then add the fennel along with the water in which it was simmering. Finally, stir in the tomato paste, bring everything to a simmer, and simmer gently, uncovered, for 30 minutes.

After that, blend it all to a purée in a food processor or blender or press through a sieve. Let cool, cover, and chill for several hours. Serve as described above, garnished with Olive Croutons and the chopped green fennel fronds.

◊

Piedmont Roasted Peppers

·

SERVES 4 AS A FIRST COURSE

This recipe is quite simply stunning: hard to imagine how something so easily prepared can taste so good. Its history is colorful too. It was first discovered by Elizabeth David and published in her splendid book Italian Food. *Then the Italian chef Franco Taruschio at the Walnut Tree Inn near Abergavenny cooked it there. Simon Hopkinson, who ate it at the Walnut Tree, put it on his menu at his great London restaurant, Bibendum, where I ate it — which is how it comes to be here now for you to make and enjoy.*

4 large red bell peppers (green are not suitable)
4 medium-sized tomatoes
8 anchovy fillets
2 cloves garlic
½ cup Italian extra-virgin olive oil
freshly ground black pepper

For this dish it is essential to use a heavy, *shallow* baking sheet, 16 × 12 inches: if the sides are too deep, the roasted vegetables won't get those lovely, nutty, toasted edges.

Preheat the oven to 350°F.

TO SERVE:
leaves from 1 small bunch fresh basil

Begin by cutting the peppers in half and removing the seeds but leaving the stems intact (they're not edible but they do look attractive, and they help the pepper halves to keep their shape). Lay the pepper halves on a lightly oiled baking sheet. Put the tomatoes in a bowl and pour boiling water over them. Leave them for 1 minute, then drain them and slip the skins off, using a cloth to protect your hands. Then cut the tomatoes in quarters and place two quarters in each pepper half.

After that, snip one anchovy fillet per pepper half into rough pieces and add to the tomatoes. Peel the garlic cloves, slice them thinly, and divide the slices equally among the tomatoes and anchovies. Now spoon some olive oil into each pepper half, season with freshly ground pepper (but no salt because of the anchovies), and place the baking sheet on a high shelf in the oven for the peppers to roast for 50 minutes to 1 hour.

Then transfer the cooked peppers to a serving dish, with all the precious juices poured over, and garnish with a few scattered basil leaves. These peppers do need good bread to go with them, as the juices are sublime. Focaccia with an olive topping (page 196) would be perfect.

——————— ◊ ———————

Piedmont Roasted Peppers

Roasted Tomato Soup *with a* Purée *of* Basil

.

SERVES 4

At first you're going to think, "Why bother to roast tomatoes just for a soup?," but I promise you that once you've tasted the difference, you'll know it's worth it — and roasting really isn't any trouble, it just means time in the oven.

1½ lbs. ripe, red tomatoes	1 teaspoon balsamic vinegar
salt and freshly ground black pepper	
about 3 tablespoons extra-virgin olive oil	**TO GARNISH:** Olive Croutons (recipe follows)
1 fat clove garlic, chopped	
leaves from 1 small bunch fresh basil	You will also need a heavy, shallow baking sheet about 13 × 13 inches.
1 medium-sized potato	
2 cups boiling water	
1½ teaspoons tomato paste	Preheat the oven to 375°F.

First of all, skin the tomatoes by pouring boiling water over them, then leaving them for 1 minute exactly before draining them and slipping off the skins (protect your hands with a cloth if necessary). Now slice each tomato in half, arrange the halves on a baking sheet, cut sides up, and season with salt and pepper. Sprinkle a few drops of olive oil onto each half, followed by the chopped garlic. Finally, top each half with a piece of basil leaf (first dipping the basil in oil to get a good coating).

Pop the whole lot into the oven and roast the tomatoes for 50 minutes to 1 hour, or until the edges are slightly blackened. What happens in this process is that the liquid in the tomatoes evaporates and the edges toast, concentrating the tomatoes' flavor. About 20 minutes before the end of the roasting time, peel and chop the potato. Place it in a saucepan with some salt, 2 cups boiling water, and the tomato paste and simmer for 20 minutes.

When the tomatoes are ready, remove them from the oven and scrape them, with all their juices and crusty bits, into a food processor (a spatula is best for this). Then add the contents of the potato saucepan and process everything to a not-too-uniform purée. If you want to, you can now sieve out the seeds, but I prefer to leave them in, as I like the texture.

Just before serving the soup — which should be reheated very gently — make the basil purée by stripping the leaves into a mortar, sprinkling with ¼ teaspoon of salt, then bashing the leaves down with the pestle. It takes a minute or two for the leaves to collapse down and become a purée, at which point add 2 tablespoons olive oil and the balsamic vinegar and stir well. (If you make this in advance, store it in a cup, tightly covered with plastic wrap so that it will keep its color even overnight.)

To serve the soup, pour it into warmed bowls and drizzle the basil purée onto the surface, giving it a marbled effect. Finally, sprinkle with Olive Croutons and serve straightaway.

———————— ◊ ————————

Olive Croutons

4 medium slices country bread	**1 tablespoon olive paste**
1½ tablespoons olive oil	
	Preheat the oven to 375°F.

First of all, cut the slices of bread into small cubes, then place them in a bowl together with the olive oil and olive paste and stir them around to get a good coating of both. Then arrange the croutons on a small baking sheet and put them in the oven to bake for 8 to 10 minutes — but please do put on a timer for this, as 10 minutes pass very quickly and croutons have a nasty habit of turning into cinders! Leave to cool on the baking sheet and serve with Chilled Fennel Gazpacho (page 3) or Roasted Tomato Soup with a Purée of Basil (page 6).

———————— ◊ ————————

Fried Halloumi Cheese
with Lime *and* Caper Vinaigrette

·

SERVES 2 AS A LIGHT LUNCH OR 4 AS A FIRST COURSE

This is a great recipe to have up your sleeve for the unexpected vegetarian. Halloumi has a reasonably long shelf life, which means that you can always have some tucked away in the refrigerator. If you can get hold of some Greek olive oil for the dressing and eat this outside in the sunshine, the scent and the flavors will transport you to the Aegean in moments.

12 ozs. halloumi cheese	1 clove garlic, finely chopped
2 tablespoons olive oil	1 teaspoon grain mustard
2 tablespoons flour seasoned with a little salt and pepper	1 tablespoon chopped fresh cilantro leaves
	2 tablespoons extra-virgin olive oil
FOR THE DRESSING:	salt and freshly ground black pepper
juice and zest of 1 lime	
1 tablespoon white wine vinegar	**TO GARNISH:**
1½ tablespoons capers, drained	a few sprigs of cilantro

First of all, pat the cheese dry with paper towels. Then, using a sharp knife, slice it into eight slices, including the ends. Now prepare the dressing by simply beating all the ingredients together in a small mixing bowl.

When you're ready to serve the halloumi, heat the oil in a skillet over medium heat. When the oil is really hot, press each slice of cheese into seasoned flour to coat it on both sides, then add it to the hot skillet — they take 1 minute on each side to cook, so by the time the last one's in, it will almost be time to turn the first one over. They need to be a good golden color on each side.

Serve them straightaway on warmed plates with the dressing poured over and garnished with the cilantro sprigs. This is good served with lightly toasted pita bread or Greek bread with toasted sesame seeds.

NOTE: Halloumi cheese is available from Lebanese, Greek, and Arabic food stores.

———————— ◊ ————————

Fried Halloumi Cheese with Lime and Caper Vinaigrette

Chilled Lemongrass *and* Cilantro Vichyssoise

·

SERVES 4

*I*n summer, if the weather is really hot, nothing could be more refreshing than a chilled soup. *If leeks, which have made this particular recipe famous, are not available in summer, this alternative is, I think, even better. It's made using fresh lemongrass, available at Asian shops. Once again, remember to serve the soup well chilled.*

2 ozs. or 1 bunch fresh cilantro	10 ozs. new potatoes, scraped and chopped small
4 thick stems lemongrass	
salt and freshly ground black pepper	⅔ cup milk
3¾ cups water	
½ stick butter	TO GARNISH:
2 medium onions, chopped	4 scallions, finely chopped
	thin lemon slices

First of all, strip the cilantro leaves from the stems and reserve the stems. Lemongrass is dealt with in exactly the same way as leeks: that is, you trim the root and the tough top away, leaving about 6 inches of stem, remove the outer skin, and chop the lemongrass quite finely. Then do the same with the scallions. Next, gather up all the trimmings, wash them, and pop them into a saucepan, together with the cilantro stems, some salt, and 3¾ cups of water. Simmer (covered) for about 30 minutes to make a stock.

To make the soup, melt the butter in a large saucepan, then add the chopped lemongrass, onions, and potatoes. Keeping the heat low, let the vegetables sweat gently (covered) for about 10 minutes. After that, pour in the stock through a strainer, discard the debris, then add the milk and about three-quarters of the cilantro leaves. Season with salt and pepper, bring the soup to a simmer, and simmer very gently for about 25 minutes.

Allow the soup to cool a little. Pour it into a food processor or blender, purée it, and then pour it through a strainer into a bowl. When it's cooled, cover and chill thoroughly till you're ready to serve. I think it's a good idea to serve the soup in glass bowls that have already been chilled. Add a cube of ice to each bowl and sprinkle in the rest of the cilantro (finely chopped) and the scallions as a garnish. Finally, float some lemon slices on top and serve straightaway.

———————— ◊ ————————

Provençale Tapenade

.

SERVES 6

In the food markets in Provence, there's always a dazzling stall piled with olives, shiny and glistening in the sun — black, green, purple, herbed, marinated, and so on. Very often, there is a tapenade stall as well, with any number of variations. Tapenade is a pungent olive paste made with anchovies and capers: perfect for outdoor eating with rough country bread and some chilled Provençale rosé.

3½ cups good-quality pitted black olives	**1 teaspoon Dijon mustard**
½ cup capers, drained and pressed between double layers of paper towels to absorb the surplus vinegar	**2 tablespoons extra-virgin olive oil**
	2 teaspoons fresh lemon juice
1 can (2 ozs.) anchovy fillets in olive oil	**2 tablespoons chopped fresh basil**
2 cloves garlic, crushed	**freshly ground black pepper**

This is very simple to make. All you do is put the olives into a food processor along with the capers. Add the contents of the can of anchovies (oil included), plus the garlic, mustard, olive oil, and lemon juice and half the basil. Blend until the mixture is reduced to a spreadable paste, but not so finely that the pieces become unidentifiable (the olives need to be chopped just enough to resemble slightly large grains of sand). Then scrape the mixture into a small bowl and taste and season with freshly ground pepper (no salt because of the anchovies). Just before serving, sprinkle in the remaining basil. Tapenade keeps for up to 2 weeks in a covered jar and can be used in a number of other ways: stir a spoonful into soup or a salad dressing, or use as a topping for baked croutons.

———————— ◊ ————————

Fresh Asparagus
with Foaming Hollandaise

·

SERVES 4 AS A FIRST COURSE

The marriage of asparagus and hollandaise was quite definitely made in heaven, and it seems sad to me that "health" issues should have brought about a divorce. Therefore, I have set out to lighten the sauce somewhat by the addition of stiffly beaten egg whites. I now actually prefer the golden foam to the classic all-butter-and-egg-yolk sauce.

FOR THE SAUCE:	1 stick salted butter
2 large eggs, separated	
salt and freshly ground black pepper	1¼ lbs. fresh asparagus stalks
2 teaspoons fresh lemon juice	(medium-thick)
2 teaspoons white wine vinegar	salt

You can make the sauce at any time: We have tried it chilled overnight in the refrigerator, which makes a nice contrast with the hot asparagus, or you can serve it warm, or even at room temperature.

Begin by placing the egg yolks in a food processor or blender together with some salt, switch on, and blend thoroughly. In a small saucepan, heat the lemon juice and vinegar till the mixture simmers, then switch the processor on again and pour the hot liquid onto the egg yolks in a steady stream.

Switch off, then in the same saucepan melt the butter — not too fiercely: it mustn't brown. When it is liquid and foaming, switch on the processor once more and pour in the butter, again in a steady, thin stream, until it is all incorporated and the sauce has thickened. Next, in a small bowl, beat the egg whites until they form soft peaks and then fold the sauce, a tablespoon at a time, into the egg whites and taste to check the seasoning. When you've done that, it's ready to be served, or you can cover and refrigerate it until you are ready to serve.

To cook the asparagus: Take each stalk in both hands and bend and snap off the woody end, then trim with a knife to make it neater. Lay the asparagus stalks on an opened basket steamer — they can be piled one on top of the other. Season with salt, place them in a skillet or saucepan, pour in about 1 inch of boiling water, cover, and steam for 4 to 6 minutes.

Serve the hot asparagus with some sauce poured over the tips, and don't forget to have finger bowls and napkins at the ready.

———————— ◊ ————————

Fresh Asparagus with Foaming Hollandaise

Sautéed Asparagus *with* Eggs *and* Parmigiano

·

SERVES 2

Asparagus has a wonderful affinity with egg and a hint of cheese, especially Parmigiano. In this recipe, it is sautéed to a nutty brown at the edges, sprinkled with a little balsamic vinegar, and served with fried eggs, though you can poach them if you prefer. If you really want to have some fun, try little fried quail's eggs, which look so pretty and dainty with their lacy brown edges. Like all eggs, though, they must be very fresh, so you need a reliable supplier. Just before serving, scatter a few shavings of Parmigiano over the dish, and you have an absolutely stunning summer lunch for two people.

1 tablespoon Parmigiano-Reggiano shavings (see recipe)	**1 tablespoon balsamic vinegar**
2 tablespoons olive oil	**2 very fresh hen's eggs or 6 quail's eggs**
8 ozs. asparagus stalks (the thinner ones are best), trimmed as in the recipe on the previous page	**salt and freshly ground black pepper**

First, prepare the Parmigiano, using a potato peeler to lightly shave off tiny slivers till you have approximately 1 tablespoon.

For this recipe you need two skillets. In the first one, heat 1 tablespoon of olive oil over a high heat, add the asparagus stalks, then immediately turn the heat down to medium. Move the stalks about in the pan and turn them so that they are a little toasted at the edges (they should take 3 to 4 minutes to cook, but this will depend on their thickness). When they're done, turn off the heat, add the balsamic vinegar, and let them keep warm in the pan while you cook the eggs.

Heat 1 tablespoon of olive oil in the other skillet. Then, if you are using quail's eggs, make a small slit in the shells with a sharp (preferably serrated) knife — if you crack them like hen's eggs, the yolks will break. When the oil is hot, quickly break the eggs into the skillet, one after the other. Then tilt the skillet and baste the eggs with hot oil, and after about 1 minute they will be done.

Arrange the asparagus on warmed plates with the pan juices sprinkled over them. Top each portion with 3 quail's eggs or 1 hen's egg, season with salt and freshly ground black pepper, sprinkle on the Parmigiano, and serve pronto.

———————— ◊ ————————

Asparagus *Under* Wraps

.

SERVES 2 AS A LIGHT LUNCH OR 4 AS A FIRST COURSE

T*he asparagus in this dish is steamed lightly, then wrapped with cheese and prosciutto and baked till the cheese is melted. Italian fontina, if you can get it, has the right squishy consistency, but the recipe also works well with the sharp flavor of Parmigiano.*

**12 asparagus stalks
(thick ones, if possible)**

**6 ozs. fontina or
Parmigiano-Reggiano**

**12 slices prosciutto, total weight
about 5 ozs.**

TO SERVE:
grated Parmigiano-Reggiano

**You will also need a heavy baking sheet,
lightly oiled.**

Preheat the oven to 400°F.

To cook the asparagus: Take each stalk in both hands and bend and snap off the woody end, then trim with a knife to make it neater. Lay the asparagus stalks on an opened basket steamer — they can be piled one on top of the other. Season with salt, place them in a skillet or saucepan, pour in about 1 inch of boiling water, cover, and steam for 4 to 6 minutes.

If you're using fontina, slice it into thin strips using a sharp knife. If you're using Parmigiano, coarsely grate it. Now lay the slices of prosciutto out flat on a work surface and divide the strips of cheese along the center of each slice (or sprinkle with the grated Parmigiano if using that). Then simply lay an asparagus stalk at one end and roll the whole lot up fairly firmly.

All this can be done well in advance; then, when you're ready to cook, lay the rolls on the baking sheet and pop onto the highest shelf of the oven for just 5 minutes, or until the cheese begins to melt. Serve piping hot, with a little grated Parmigiano to sprinkle over.

◊

CHAPTER TWO

Salads
and
DRESSINGS

◇

When I first started writing recipes, the postwar British salad was still being heavily laced with bottled salad dressing. Not so now. Salad leaves daily get more and more exotic, and oils and vinegars come in every shape, size, and flavor. You can buy Greek olive oil to go in a Greek dish — or French, Italian, or Spanish likewise. Then there are herb oils and fruit vinegars, a bewildering array and — dare I say it? — a little over the top for most of us. Unless I'm regularly making a recipe that calls for, say, strawberry vinegar, all it does is sit there taking up valuable room awaiting the special need that never arises. After some early-summer experiments with a whole range of herb-infused oils, I then found that they stood around almost never used (the only exception being basil oil, which came into its own in winter when there was no basil to be had). One of the glories of summer is the profusion of herbs, so if you want their flavor, use them fresh — there's no need for oils.

For something new in salads, can I urge you to try the Pesto Rice Salad (page 28), a cross between a salad and a risotto? Another winner is the Grilled Spanish Onion with Arugula Salad (page 26), and the Mixed-Leaf Caesar Salad on page 20 is, I may say with all modesty, the best I've tasted to date!

Middle Eastern Tabbouleh Salad

.

SERVES 6 TO 8 AS A SIDE SALAD

*T*his Middle Eastern salad is very pretty and summery, and if you have mint in the garden that is growing as wild as a jungle — as mine does — it's a wonderful way to use some of it!

1½ cups medium-grain bulgur	1½ cups fresh mint leaves, finely chopped
2 cups parsley, finely chopped	
8 scallions, finely chopped (including the green parts)	4 inches cucumber, very finely chopped
⅓ cup fresh lemon juice	⅓ cup extra-virgin olive oil
salt and freshly ground black pepper	
2 large beefsteak tomatoes, about 1 lb.	TO SERVE: crisp lettuce leaves

Place the bulgur in a bowl, cover it with plenty of cold water, and leave it for about 20 minutes, or until the grains soften and lose their crunchiness (which means, of course, you'll have to bite a few to find out how they're going).

Then have ready a large sieve or colander lined with a clean dish towel. When the bulgur has softened, pour the contents of the bowl into the sieve, drain, and squeeze hard to extract as much water as possible. Shake the wheat into a deep bowl and stir in the parsley and scallions, followed by the lemon juice and 1½ teaspoons of salt, to combine thoroughly. Then (if you have time) chill it in the refrigerator for 1 hour.

Meanwhile, skin the tomatoes. Pour boiling water over them and leave them for 1 minute, then slip off the skins, protecting your hands with a cloth if you need to. Halve the tomatoes and squeeze out the seeds before chopping the flesh quite small and adding it to the bowl containing the wheat. Next, add the mint, cucumber, and olive oil to the salad and mix to combine everything. Taste and season with salt and pepper. Serve piled on a plate lined with some crisp lettuce leaves.

◊

Mixed-Leaf Caesar Salad

.

SERVES 4 AS A LIGHT LUNCH OR 6 AS A FIRST COURSE

This must be one of the greatest salad recipes ever. It's traditionally made with Romaine lettuce, but I like to add some arugula leaves. What it can't take is anything too soft — only the crunchiest lettuce leaves will do. The flavors are gutsy, so it's ideal for a summer lunch outside or, in small portions, for a quite aristocratic but so-simple first course.

FOR THE CROUTONS:

2 slices white bread, crusts removed, cut into ⅓-inch cubes

1 tablespoon extra-virgin olive oil

1½ tablespoons finely grated Parmigiano-Reggiano

1 clove garlic, crushed

FOR THE DRESSING:

1 large egg

1 clove garlic

juice of 1 lime

1½ teaspoons mustard powder

½ teaspoon Worcestershire sauce

⅔ cup extra-virgin olive oil

salt and freshly ground black pepper

½ cup Parmigiano-Reggiano, finely grated

1 large Romaine lettuce

1 large handful arugula

1 can (2 ozs.) anchovy fillets, drained (keep the oil for the dressing)

You will also need a baking sheet.

First make the croutons: Preheat the oven to 350°F, then place the cubes of bread in a bowl, together with 1 tablespoon olive oil and 1½ tablespoons cheese, plus the crushed clove of garlic. Stir and toss the bread around to get an even coating of cheese, oil, and garlic, then spread the croutons out on the baking sheet and bake them on a high shelf in the oven for 10 minutes. Please put a kitchen timer on at this stage! I'm afraid I have burnt more croutons than I care to remember simply because the 10 minutes went so quickly! When the buzzer goes off, remove them from the oven and leave to cool.

Meanwhile, make the dressing: Break the egg into the bowl of a food processor. Add the garlic (peeled but not crushed), the lime juice, 2 of the anchovy fillets, the mustard, and the Worcestershire sauce. Switch on and blend everything till smooth; then, keeping the motor running, pour the olive oil and anchovy oil through the feed tube in a slow, steady stream.

When all the oil is in, you should have a slightly thickened, emulsified sauce with the consistency of heavy cream. Taste the dressing and season with freshly ground black pepper and salt if needed. Cover and refrigerate until ready to serve.

(continued on page 22)

Mixed-Leaf Caesar Salad

Now arrange the lettuce leaves (breaking up the larger ones as you go) and the arugula in a large, roomy salad bowl. Snip in the remaining anchovies and mix to distribute them evenly among the leaves. When you're ready to serve, pour the dressing over the leaves and toss very thoroughly to coat all the leaves. Sprinkle in the Parmigiano, toss again, and finally scatter the croutons over the salad. Then either divide into portions or pass the bowl around for everyone to help themselves.

◇

Pita Bread Salad

.

SERVES 4 AS A MAIN COURSE OR 6 AS A SIDE SALAD WITH BARBECUED MEAT OR FISH

Another Middle Eastern salad, originally called fattoush, *this may sound unlikely, but it really is good. It's robust and chunky with the fresh flavors of herbs and lemon — and dead simple to make.*

1 small Romaine lettuce, cut into ½-inch strips	1 cup coarsely chopped parsley
2 largish tomatoes, skinned and cut into ½-inch cubes	¼ cup snipped fresh mint leaves
4 inches unpeeled cucumber, cut into ½-inch cubes	FOR THE LEMON DRESSING:
4 scallions, thinly sliced (including the green parts)	⅔ cup olive oil
1 smallish red onion, chopped fine	zest of 1 lemon
1 red, yellow, or green bell pepper, deseeded and chopped fine	⅓ cup fresh lemon juice
	salt and freshly ground black pepper
	2 pita breads

Preheat the broiler to its highest setting.

In a large, roomy salad bowl, combine the vegetables and chopped herbs and toss lightly to mix them evenly together. Then in another small bowl, combine the ingredients for the dressing, beat, and season liberally. Spoon the dressing over the salad and toss again.

Now toast the pita bread under the broiler until it starts to get really crisp. Cut it into postage-stamp-sized pieces, scatter these into the salad, and toss once more. Taste for seasoning and serve immediately.

◊

Roasted Tomato Salad

·

SERVES 4 TO 6 AS A FIRST COURSE

If you are a tomato addict, like me, and you think that good bread dipped into fruity olive oil and tomato juices is the food of the gods, then roast the tomatoes first and you'll agree that the gods have surpassed themselves.

12 large tomatoes
salt and freshly ground black pepper
2 large or 4 small cloves garlic, finely chopped
2 tablespoons extra-virgin olive oil
12 large fresh basil leaves

FOR THE DRESSING:
2 tablespoons extra-virgin olive oil

2 tablespoons balsamic vinegar

TO GARNISH:
12 large fresh basil leaves
24 black olives

You will also need a shallow roasting pan about 16 × 12 inches, oiled.

Preheat the oven to 400°F.

First, skin the tomatoes: Pour boiling water over them and leave them for 1 minute, then drain, and as soon as they are cool enough to handle, slip off the skins. (Protect your hands with a cloth if necessary.) Now cut each tomato in half, place the halves in the roasting pan (cut sides up), and season with salt and freshly ground pepper. After that, sprinkle on the chopped garlic, distributing it evenly among the tomatoes. Follow this with a few drops of olive oil on each one, then top each one with half a basil leaf, turning each piece of leaf over to get a coating of oil.

Now place the roasting pan in the top half of the oven and roast the tomatoes for 50 minutes to 1 hour, or until the edges are slightly blackened. Then remove the pan from the oven and allow the tomatoes to cool. All this can be done several hours ahead.

To serve the tomatoes, transfer them to individual plates, place half a basil leaf on top of each tomato half, then beat the oil and balsamic vinegar together and drizzle this over the tomatoes. Finally, top each one with an olive. Lots of crusty bread is an essential accompaniment to this dish.

———————— ◊ ————————

Roasted Tomato Salad

Grilled Spanish Onion *with* Arugula Salad

.

SERVES 4

I am constantly amazed after all my years of cooking at how there can be anything new — but there always is, and again and again. This is an example, utterly simple, yet quite unlike any other salad. If arugula is unavailable, a combination of flat-leaf parsley and mâche is a good substitute.

4 Spanish onions	**juice of 1 large lemon**
½ cup extra-virgin olive oil	
salt and freshly ground black pepper	**You will also need a broiler pan lined with foil with a rack on top.**
1 piece (3 ozs.) Parmigiano-Reggiano	
½ bunch arugula or 1 oz. mixed flat-leaf parsley and mâche	Preheat the broiler at its highest setting for about 5 minutes.

First of all, don't peel the onions: simply trim off the root and top before cutting each one across into four circular slices about ¾ inch thick. Keeping the slices whole, transfer them to the broiler pan (you might have to do this in two batches, depending on the size of your broiler), then brush them with oil and season with salt and freshly ground pepper. Now position the pan so that the onion slices are about 4 inches from the heat and broil 7–8 minutes, or until the onions are browned — indeed, within a whisker of being blackened.

While that's happening, prepare the Parmigiano by shaving it into wafer-thin pieces with a potato peeler. For the onions, the next stage needs a little care: use a spatula to turn the slices over so that they don't break up into their constituent rings. Repeat the same oiling, seasoning, and broiling on the other side, then remove from the heat and set aside until they're cool enough to handle.

Now discard the outside layers and any parts of the onion slices that are too blackened or chewy to eat, and separate the cold onions into rings. Put about a quarter of the rings in a layer on a serving dish and gradually build up the salad, intermingling onion rings with the torn arugula and shavings of Parmigiano, sprinkling with more salt and pepper, lemon juice, and the remaining olive oil as you go. This salad should not be tossed, so it relies on the cook to mingle the ingredients as the salad is put together. Serve at room temperature.

———————— ◊ ————————

Homemade Pesto Sauce

.

SERVES 2 TO 3 WITH PASTA

Every year I grow enough basil leaves to see me through the summer and, most important, to make at least one homemade pesto sauce. A lot of precious leaves are needed to make up two ounces of sauce, but it really is worth it, as the homemade version puts all the ready-made ones in the shade. Pecorino Romano has a more gutsy flavor than Parmigiano, but if you can't get it, Parmigiano will do well.

2 cups fresh basil leaves	½ cup extra-virgin olive oil
1 large clove garlic, crushed	salt
1½ tablespoons pine nuts	⅓ cup Pecorino Romano, grated

If you have a blender, put the basil, garlic, pine nuts, and olive oil together with some salt in the blender and blend until you have a smooth purée. Then transfer the purée to a bowl and stir in the grated Pecorino.

If you don't have a blender, use a large mortar and pestle to pound the basil, garlic, and pine nuts to a paste. Slowly add the salt and cheese, then very gradually add the oil until you have obtained a smooth purée.

———— ◊ ————

Pesto Rice Salad

·

SERVES 4 TO 6 AS A FIRST COURSE

*J*ust as homemade pesto does such wonders for pasta, so it does for rice too. This salad can be served warm as a first course, and it's extremely good as an accompaniment to fish or chicken main-course dishes. Served cold, it makes a lovely addition to a selection of salads for a buffet.

1 recipe Homemade Pesto Sauce (see previous page)	**juice of 1 lemon**
1 cup Italian arborio rice	**2 tablespoons extra-virgin olive oil**
2 cups boiling chicken or vegetable stock	**a few fresh basil leaves**
salt and freshly ground black pepper	**4 scallions, finely chopped**
	½ cup Parmigiano-Reggiano shavings (made with a potato peeler)

Add about one-quarter of the pesto sauce to the rice and stir it around to coat all the grains. Tip the mixture into either a shallow saucepan or a skillet with a lid and pour the boiling stock over the rice. Now turn on the heat to high and stir with a wooden spoon, adding 1 teaspoon of salt. Then, when it begins to boil, put a lid on, turn the heat down to low, and let the rice cook for exactly 20 minutes.

As soon as it's ready, tip all the rice into a serving bowl, then simply pour in the lemon juice, the olive oil, and the remaining pesto sauce and combine, stirring and tossing. At this stage, taste and season with salt and pepper. Finally, scatter some torn basil leaves, the finely chopped scallions, and some shavings of Parmigiano over the surface of the salad as a garnish. If you want to serve the salad cold, don't add the basil, scallions, and Parmigiano until just before serving.

———————— ◊ ————————

Pesto Rice Salad

Marinated Mozzarella *with* Avocado

·

SERVES 2 AS A LIGHT LUNCH

This is very pretty and very summery, but it is dependent on getting hold of good-quality, absolutely fresh mozzarella. Buffalo mozzarella is the best, but failing that, the full-fat cheese made with cow's milk has a lovely creamy texture.

4 ozs. mozzarella	**½ teaspoon coarse salt**
1 medium-sized ripe avocado	**salt and freshly ground black pepper**
strip of red bell pepper, 1 × 3 inches	**1½ teaspoons mustard powder**
about 18 fresh basil leaves	**2 teaspoons white wine vinegar**
2 scallions, finely chopped	**¼ cup extra-virgin olive oil**
	2 teaspoons snipped fresh chives
FOR THE VINAIGRETTE DRESSING:	
1 small clove garlic	

Start to prepare the salad about 2 hours before you need it (but no longer, as the cheese then begins to soften too much). Slice the mozzarella into ¼-inch slices; then halve the avocado, remove and discard the pit and skin, and thinly slice each half.

Arrange the mozzarella and avocado on a platter with alternate slices overlapping each other. Next, slice the strip of red pepper into the finest shreds possible, starting from the narrow, 1-inch end. Then pile the basil leaves on top of one another, slice these into similar shreds, and scatter the scallions, basil, and pepper over the cheese and avocado.

Make the dressing by crushing the garlic and salt together with a mortar and pestle and work the mustard into the puréed garlic and salt, followed by plenty of freshly ground pepper. Stir in the vinegar, oil, and chives, then pour the dressing into a screw-top jar and shake vigorously before pouring it over the other ingredients on the plate. Cover with an upturned plate or some foil and leave to marinate for 2 hours. Serve with focaccia.

———————— ◊ ————————

Tomato, Mozzarella, *and* Basil Salad

.

SERVES 2

If you don't have time for a marinade, as in the previous recipe, this variation makes a very quick, simple first course or light lunch salad.

1 lb. tomatoes	**salt and freshly ground black pepper**
4 ozs. mozzarella, sliced	**2 tablespoons Italian extra-virgin**
about 24 fresh basil leaves	**olive oil**

First, put the tomatoes in a bowl and pour boiling water over them. Leave them for 1 minute, then drain and slip the skins off, using a cloth to protect your hands if necessary. Then slice the tomatoes thinly.

All you do now is arrange the slices of mozzarella and tomato in layers, either in rows or concentric circles, on a platter. Scatter the basil leaves over them; then, just before serving, sprinkle with plenty of salt and freshly ground pepper and drizzle the olive oil all over. Serve with some warm focaccia.

———————— ◊ ————————

Fresh Crab Salad in Vinaigrette

.

SERVES 2

*T*his is a very good recipe, as the tartness of capers, cornichons, and lime cuts through the richness of the crab perfectly.

8 ozs. prepared fresh lump or backfin crab meat	**1 shallot, finely chopped**
2 large or 4 small cornichons, finely chopped	**1 tablespoon white wine**
1 tablespoon capers, drained, chopped if large	**1 tablespoon light olive oil**
1 tablespoon finely chopped fresh cilantro leaves	**a few drops of Tabasco**
	salt and freshly ground black pepper
finely grated zest of 1 lime	**TO GARNISH:**
2 tablespoons fresh lime juice	**a few crisp salad leaves or some watercress**

It couldn't be simpler: All you do is combine all the ingredients in a bowl, then divide the mixture into two. Take each quantity, pile it on a plate, and use your hands to form it into a round, flattened shape about ½ inch high. Garnish with some crisp salad leaves all around and serve with some buttered brown bread. The Whole-Grain Bread with Sunflower and Poppy Seeds on page 201 goes particularly well with this.

———————— ◊ ————————

Blue Cheese Dressing

SERVES 4 TO 6

I have a great weakness for blue cheese salad dressing. You can either use Roquefort, if you want to go all out, or Danish Blue, which crumbles well: the only stipulation is that the cheese has to be gutsy. A subtle, fainthearted cheese will get lost among all the other strong flavors.

1 large or 2 small cloves garlic	⅔ cup sour cream
1 teaspoon salt	2 tablespoons good mayonnaise
1½ teaspoons mustard powder	2 scallions, finely chopped
1 tablespoon fresh lemon juice	½ cup blue cheese, crumbled
1 tablespoon balsamic vinegar	freshly ground black pepper
2 tablespoons light olive oil	

Start off by crushing the garlic clove together with 1 teaspoon salt down to a creamy mass in a mortar and pestle. Next, add the mustard and work it in. Next add the lemon juice and vinegar, and after that the oil and mix everything together thoroughly. Then in a bowl combine the sour cream and mayonnaise and gradually beat into the dressing ingredients. When all is thoroughly blended, add the chopped scallions and the crumbled blue cheese. Season with freshly ground pepper. The dressing is now ready to use. A few crunchy Olive Croutons (page 7) are a nice addition when you come to dress the salad.

——————— ◊ ———————

Balsamic Vinaigrette Dressing

.

MAKES ENOUGH FOR A SALAD FOR 6 PEOPLE

B*alsamic vinegar, which is now widely available, has done wonders for the modern cookery repertoire, imparting its rich, dark, distinctive flavor to many dishes. In vinaigrette it really comes into its fullest glory.*

1 fat clove garlic	**freshly ground black pepper**
1 teaspoon coarse salt	**1 tablespoon balsamic vinegar**
1½ teaspoons mustard powder	**⅓ cup extra-virgin olive oil**

A mortar and pestle is indispensable for making vinaigrette. All you do is peel a clove of garlic, pop it into the bowl, along with the salt, and smash the garlic with the pestle. As the garlic breaks down and mingles with the salt, it will turn very quickly into a creamy mass. Now add the mustard and several good grinds of pepper and work these into the garlic. Next, mix in first the vinegar and then the oil, and when everything's amalgamated, pour the whole lot into a small screw-top jar until you're ready to serve the salad. Give it a hefty shake before using.

NOTE: Don't make vinaigrette too far in advance — it's best made not more than an hour or so before you need it.

———————— ◊ ————————

CHAPTER THREE

SUMMER FISH *and* SHELLFISH

---◊---

It is a paradox that just as the decline in the number of fish markets is reaching alarming proportions, fish is beginning to assume a more and more important role in our diet. There is a growing number — not least among my own family and friends — of what I call "semi-veggies": that is, people who won't eat meat but who *do* eat fish and are constantly calling for new ideas and recipes.

Happily, the quality and variety of fish available in supermarkets has improved greatly in recent years, but there is still one deficiency that distresses me, and that is the short supply of natural (not farmed) salmon that migrate to the rivers from the sea and have had the benefit of a traditional diet of crustaceans, which give it its highly prized flavor. Young people are rarely excited by salmon simply because they have most often, if not always, tasted indifferent farmed fish rather than the real thing. It need not be so. I have tasted farmed salmon from Norway that was excellent, so there is hope.

Meanwhile, my suggestion is to try once each summer to get hold of the real thing — expensive but worth it — and to use one of the several recipes in this chapter, all of which are expressly devised to keep in that glorious flavor while cooking.

Salmon Rösti Fish Cakes

.

SERVES 4 AS A MAIN COURSE OR 8 AS A FIRST COURSE

I've got a thing about fish cakes: if ever they appear on a restaurant menu, I always order them — and I'm frequently trying to dream up new variations. This one is a real winner. You can make it with any fish: it doesn't have to be salmon. Serve them with Toasted Corn Salsa (page 42), which is a cross between a sauce and a salad, low in calories, and absolutely delicious.

8 ozs. firm-fleshed new potatoes	**2 tablespoons fresh lime juice**
salt	**2 tablespoons chopped fresh cilantro**
12 ozs. tail end of salmon (ask your fish market to remove the skin and bones)	**a couple of pinches of cayenne pepper**
	peanut oil for frying
1½ tablespoons capers, drained, roughly chopped if large	**TO GARNISH:**
	sprigs of fresh cilantro

Begin by washing the potatoes, then place them in a saucepan (skins on), add salt, and just cover with boiling water. Cover the pan and boil for 10 minutes.

Meanwhile, chop the salmon into chunks and give it a few pulses in a food processor to chop it fairly finely (or you can do this by hand). Place the salmon in a mixing bowl and add the capers, lime juice, and chopped cilantro leaves. Mix well and season with salt and cayenne. When the potatoes have had their 10 minutes, they won't be cooked through, but that's how we want them. Drain them, and when they are cool enough to handle, peel off the skins and grate them, using the coarse blade of a grater. Then carefully combine them with the salmon, trying not to break up the grated bits.

Now take tablespoons of the mixture and slap them into cakes: you need to press the mixture firmly together, but don't worry about the ragged edges because these look pretty when they cook. Repeat until the mixture is used up: you should have twelve cakes. Measure 1 to 2 tablespoons of oil into a skillet, and when the oil is really hot, add the fish cakes. Fry them for 3 minutes on each side to a crusty golden color. Drain on paper towels as they leave the pan, and serve garnished with sprigs of cilantro and accompanied by Toasted Corn Salsa (page 42).

◊

Rösti Crab Cakes

·

SERVES 2 AS MAIN COURSE OR 4 AS A FIRST COURSE

As a great lover of any type of fish cake, I have always adored American crab cakes. In this recipe, the potato counteracts the richness of the crab more effectively than the usual breadcrumbs, and when these are served with Pickled Limes (page 184), you will have a marriage made in heaven!

5 ozs. firm waxy potatoes	**2 pinches of cayenne pepper**
salt and freshly ground black pepper	**1½ tablespoons chopped fresh cilantro or parsley**
8 ozs. prepared fresh lump or backfin crabmeat, finely shredded	**peanut oil for frying**
1½ tablespoons capers, drained, chopped if large	
1 tablespoon fresh lime juice	**TO GARNISH:**
1 teaspoon grated lime zest	**lime quarters**
2 finely chopped scallions (including the green parts)	**sprigs of fresh cilantro or flat-leaf parsley**

First, put the unpeeled potatoes in a saucepan with boiling water and salt and simmer them for exactly 10 minutes. Meanwhile, place the rest of the ingredients in a mixing bowl and mix together thoroughly. When the potatoes are cooked, drain them, and as soon as they are cool enough to handle, peel off the skins and grate the flesh on the coarse blade of a grater, pushing the potatoes all the way down the length of it so that the strips are as long as possible.

Now carefully combine the grated potato with the crab mixture, trying not to break up the pieces of potato. Have a tray or baking sheet handy. Take rough tablespoons of the mixture and form them into eight little cakes, squeezing and pressing them evenly together. Don't worry about any ragged edges: this is precisely what gives the crab cakes their charm when cooked.

When the cakes are made, cover them with plastic wrap and leave in the refrigerator for at least 2 hours to chill and become firm. To cook, heat 1½ tablespoons of oil in a skillet, making sure it is very hot, then gently slide in the crab cakes using a spatula. Cook them for 3 minutes on each side, turning the heat down to medium. Don't turn them over until the 3 minutes are up or they will not be firm enough. Remove them to a plate lined with paper towels, then transfer to a warmed platter and garnish with lime quarters and cilantro or parsley. Serve with Pickled Limes (page 184) or with Toasted Corn Salsa (page 42) or Avocado Salsa (page 43).

◊

Rösti Crab Cakes

Toasted Corn Salsa

SERVES 4

I f *possible, make this salsa at least half an hour before you serve it to allow the flavors to develop.*

2 ears of corn, stripped of husks and silk	**2 large firm tomatoes, skinned, deseeded, and chopped**
a little olive oil	**2 tablespoons chopped fresh cilantro**
½ red bell pepper, very finely chopped	**2 tablespoons fresh lime juice**
½ medium-sized red onion, finely chopped	**a few drops of Tabasco**
	salt and freshly ground black pepper

Preheat the broiler to its highest setting, then rub the corn kernels with a trace of olive oil. Place them under the broiler and toast them for about 8 minutes, turning them from time to time so that they toast evenly. When they're cool enough to handle, hold each one firmly with a cloth and scrape off all the kernels using your sharpest knife. Then mix these together with all the other ingredients, taste to check the seasoning, and serve with the Salmon Rösti Fish Cakes (page 39).

◊

Avocado Salsa

.

SERVES 4

This avocado salsa — *a cross between a sauce and a salad* — *not only complements the flavor of salmon, but it also looks pretty against the pink of the fish.*

2 large, firm tomatoes	**2 tablespoons fresh lime juice**
1 ripe but firm avocado	**a few drops of Tabasco**
½ small red onion	**salt and freshly ground**
1½ tablespoons chopped fresh cilantro	**black pepper**

Skin the tomatoes by pouring boiling water over them, leaving them for exactly 1 minute before draining, and slipping the skins off when they're cool enough to handle. Cut each tomato in half, and holding each half over a saucer (cut side down), squeeze gently to extract the seeds. Now chop the tomato flesh as finely as possible.

Next, halve the avocado, remove the pit, cut each half into quarters, and peel off the skin. Chop the avocado into minutely small dice, and do the same with the onion. Finally, combine all the salsa ingredients in a bowl. Cover with plastic wrap and set aside for an hour before serving to allow the flavors to develop.

Serve this salsa with either grilled or baked salmon or the Salmon Rösti Fish Cakes (page 39).

———————— ◊ ————————

Salmon *with a* Saffron Couscous Crust

·

SERVES 4

This is unusual, but it works like a dream and is very simple to prepare. The couscous crust encases the salmon and keeps all the fragrant juices inside intact. Served with the Tomato and Olive Vinaigrette (next recipe) and perhaps some fresh shelled peas, it makes a perfect main course for summer entertaining.

¾ cup couscous
¾ cup dry white wine
2 to 3 good pinches of saffron threads
salt and freshly ground black pepper
4 boned and skinned fillets of salmon, 5 ozs. each

1 egg, beaten

You will also need a baking sheet, lightly greased.

Preheat the oven to 375°F.

First of all, prepare the couscous — which is dead simple. All you do is place it in a bowl, then heat up the wine in a saucepan till it begins to simmer. Stir the saffron into it, along with some salt and pepper, and pour the whole lot over the couscous grains. Set the couscous aside until it has absorbed all the liquid. After this, fluff it by making cutting movements across and through it with a knife.

Take each salmon fillet and season it with salt and pepper. Dip it first into beaten egg, then sit it on top of the couscous, and using your hands, coat it on all sides, pressing the couscous evenly all around (it works in just the same way as breadcrumbs). Now place the coated fillets on the baking sheet, and if you want, cover with plastic wrap and refrigerate until needed. When you are ready to cook, pop them into the preheated oven and bake for 15 to 20 minutes, or a little longer if the fish is very thick. Serve each one in a pool of Tomato and Olive Vinaigrette and serve the rest of the vinaigrette separately.

———————— ◊ ————————

Tomato *and* Olive Vinaigrette

1 fat clove garlic	**2 medium-sized tomatoes, skinned, deseeded, and chopped small**
coarse salt and freshly ground black pepper	**⅔ cup pitted black olives, chopped to the same size as the tomatoes**
1 teaspoon grain mustard	
1 tablespoon white wine vinegar	
1 tablespoon fresh lemon juice	**1 tablespoon chopped fresh chervil or flat-leaf parsley**
½ cup olive oil	

Crush the garlic with 1 teaspoon of coarse salt, using a mortar and pestle, then add the mustard, vinegar, lemon juice, and olive oil and a good seasoning of black pepper, and mix thoroughly. About half an hour before serving, add the tomatoes, olives, and chopped chervil.

◊

Salmon Steaks *with* Avocado *and* Crème Fraîche Sauce

·

SERVES 6

If you want to serve something really special for a summer dinner party that leaves you utterly free from any hassle, this cold salmon dish fills the bill perfectly. Although this recipe serves six, you can in fact line up the salmon steaks in any number you like — twelve or even twenty-four — which makes it ideal for buffet parties and celebrations.

FOR THE SALMON:

6 fresh salmon steaks, weighing about 6 ozs. each

6 small sprigs of fresh tarragon

2 bay leaves

salt and freshly ground black pepper

⅓ cup dry white wine

FOR THE SAUCE:

1 good-sized avocado

1 small clove garlic, peeled

1 teaspoon sherry vinegar

salt and freshly ground black pepper

8 ozs. crème fraîche

TO GARNISH:

1 bunch watercress or other pretty leaves

Preheat the oven to 350°F.

First of all, take a large sheet of foil (about 36 × 24 inches) and lay it in a shallow baking pan. Wipe the pieces of salmon with paper towels and place each one on the foil. Now put a small sprig of tarragon on top of each one, along with a piece of bay leaf (these ingredients are there simply to perfume the salmon very subtly without altering its flavor).

Season with salt and freshly ground pepper and finally spoon a little wine over each salmon steak before wrapping the whole lot loosely in the foil. Make a pleat in the top to seal it. Place the foil parcel on a highish shelf in the oven for exactly 20 minutes. Then remove the pan from the oven and let the salmon cool inside the foil without opening it.

Meanwhile, prepare the sauce: Halve the avocado, remove the pit, then divide into quarters and peel off the skin, using a sharp knife if necessary. Place the flesh in a blender or food processor. Then, using a teaspoon, scrape the avocado skin to remove the last, greenest part and add that in as well.

Now pop in the garlic clove, then measure in the sherry vinegar, add salt and pepper, and blend until smooth. Next, remove the purée to a mixing bowl and simply fold in the crème fraîche till it's thoroughly blended. Taste to check the seasoning — it might need a spot more vinegar. Cover the bowl with plastic wrap and keep in the refrigerator until you're ready to serve. This should be made only a few hours in advance to keep the luscious green color at its best.

When you're ready to serve the salmon, undo the foil, and using a sharp knife, ease off the strip of skin around the edge of each steak and discard it.

Remove the herbs, then transfer the fish to a platter and decorate with small bunches of watercress. Hand the sauce around separately.

NOTE: If you prefer, you can cook salmon fillets in exactly the same way, using 5-ounce fillets and cooking them for only 10 to 15 minutes.

———————— ◊ ————————

Hot *and* Sour Pickled Shrimp

.

SERVES 4 AS A FIRST COURSE

This is an ace of a first course for busy people. It is dead easy to prepare, and as it needs at least 48 hours to pickle the jumbo shrimp and allow the flavors to develop, there's absolutely nothing to do at the last minute. You can, if you want, use smaller shrimp (or even the ready-peeled frozen kind). Please don't worry about including Tabasco in the marinade — it really doesn't make it fiery-hot but gives it what I'd call a lively piquancy.

16 jumbo shrimp	**½ tablespoon Worcestershire sauce**
1 tablespoon drained capers	**½ tablespoon Tabasco**
½ medium-sized yellow bell pepper, very thinly sliced	**½ teaspoon salt**
	freshly ground black pepper
½ medium-sized red bell pepper, very thinly sliced	**1 teaspoon sugar**
1 small red onion, thinly sliced	**TO GARNISH:**
½ lemon, thinly sliced	**sprigs of cilantro**
⅔ cup light olive oil	**½ lime, thinly sliced**
1 teaspoon mustard powder	
¼ cup cider vinegar	**You will also need a 2-pint-capacity**
juice of 2 limes	**nonmetallic dish or plastic storage box.**

To prepare the shrimp, remove the shells and heads (if there are any) but leave the tails on, as they look very attractive. Then use the tip of a small sharp knife to cut a slit all along the back of each shrimp and remove the black thread that sometimes runs from head to tail. Place the shrimp and capers in the dish, together with the sliced peppers, onion, and lemon.

Now in a bowl or jar mix the oil, mustard, vinegar, lime juice, Worcestershire sauce, and Tabasco together, adding the salt, a little coarsely ground black pepper, and the sugar. Pour this mixture all over the shrimp, cover the container, and place it in the refrigerator for at least 48 hours, giving the contents a shake or stirring them around from time to time.

Serve the shrimp garnished with sprigs of cilantro and slices of lime and drenched with plenty of the marinade. You should have lots of bread on hand to mop up the juices.

———————— ◊ ————————

Hot and Sour Pickled Shrimp

Fried Skate Wings
with Warm Green Salsa

·

SERVES 2

Skate wings have everything going for them. They have a fine-flavored, creamy flesh that comes away from the bone with no fuss or bother, and they're dead easy to cook. I love them shallow-fried to a crisp golden color, with the following sharp, lemony, and quite gutsy sauce poured in at the last moment. Serve with a mixture of dressed green salad leaves and with some tiny new potatoes.

FOR THE GREEN SALSA:	⅓ cup fresh lime juice
1 medium-sized clove garlic	freshly ground black pepper
½ teaspoon coarse salt	
4 anchovy fillets, drained and finely chopped	
1½ tablespoons capers, drained	FOR THE SKATE:
1½ teaspoons grain mustard	1 lb. skate wings (2 small or 1 large cut in half)
1 tablespoon chopped fresh basil	
2 tablespoons chopped flat-leaf parsley	1½ tablespoons flour, seasoned with a little salt and pepper
2 tablespoons olive oil	2 tablespoons oil

I think it's preferable to make the sauce not too far ahead, as the parsley tends to discolor, though you could make up most of the sauce in advance and add the parsley at the last moment — either way, it's very quick and easy. All you do is crush a clove of garlic with ½ teaspoon of salt, using a mortar and pestle (or using the back of a tablespoon on a board), till you get a pastelike consistency. Then simply combine this with all the other sauce ingredients and mix everything very thoroughly.

To cook the skate wings: Take a 10-inch skillet and put it on a gentle heat to warm up while you wipe the fish with paper towels and then coat it with a light dusting of seasoned flour. Now turn the heat up to high, add the oil to the skillet, and as soon as it's really hot, add the skate wings.

Fry them for about 4 to 5 minutes on each side, depending on their size and thickness — slide the tip of a sharp knife in and push to see if the flesh parts from the bone easily and looks creamy white. Then pour in the sauce all around the fish to heat very briefly. It doesn't need to cook but simply to warm a little. Serve the fish straightaway with the sauce spooned over.

NOTE: This sauce works well with fried cod steaks or any other fried fish.

———————— ◊ ————————

Thai Red Curry Paste

·

MAKES 8 TABLESPOONS (ABOUT ⅔ CUP)

This dark, pungent curry paste makes a delightful alternative to ground dry spices. I have included it in the shrimp recipe on page 53, the fish cake recipe on page 52, and the chicken recipe on page 116, so it's best to make it in bulk, freeze it, and use it as and when you need it. It freezes really well, which means that you don't have to shop for small amounts of the ingredients — which may take some finding.

4 medium red chilies	**4 stems lemongrass, trimmed and**
4 teaspoons coriander seeds	**chopped (see page 10)**
2 teaspoons cumin seeds	**4 shallots, peeled**
1½ tablespoons hot paprika	**6 cloves garlic**
2 teaspoons grated fresh ginger	**grated zest and juice of 2 limes**

Begin by splitting the chilies in half and removing and discarding the seeds. After that wash your hands, because the seeds are very fiery, and if you touch the delicate skin on your face after handling them it can smart and burn. (I've done it so often!) Take a small skillet and preheat it over a medium heat, then add the coriander and cumin seeds and toss them around in the dry skillet to roast them and draw out their flavors. After about 5 minutes, tip them into a mortar and crush them finely to a powder.

Now simply place the chilies, the spices, and all the other ingredients in a food processor and purée to a coarse paste. Then measure out the quantity you need and freeze the rest in 2-tablespoon portions. Don't forget to label and date. It will keep for 2 months.

—————— ◊ ——————

Thai Fish Cakes
with Cucumber Dipping Sauce

·

SERVES 2 AS A MAIN COURSE OR 4 AS A FIRST COURSE

If you have some red curry paste on hand (see page 51), these little fish cakes make a wonderfully different first course, especially if the rest of the meal has a spicy theme.

16 ozs. any white fish (cod, haddock, etc.), weighed after boning and skinning, then cut into chunks	FOR THE CUCUMBER DIPPING SAUCE:
	2 inches unpeeled cucumber
2 tablespoons fresh cilantro leaves	2 shallots
	1 small carrot
1 tablespoon fresh lime juice	1 small green chili, deseeded
2 scallions, very finely sliced (including the green parts)	1 teaspoon grated fresh ginger
	1½ tablespoons roasted peanuts
2 tablespoons Thai Red Curry Paste (page 51)	1 tablespoon soft light brown sugar
	½ cup rice vinegar or wine vinegar
1 green chili, deseeded	1 tablespoon light soy sauce
salt	1 tablespoon peanut oil
2 tablespoons peanut oil for frying	
	TO GARNISH:
	sprigs of fresh cilantro

Simply place the chunks of fish, cilantro leaves, lime juice, scallions, curry paste, and chili, and a little salt, in a food processor and blend till you have a finely minced texture — don't blend it to a fine purée, though, as this is not so good. Transfer to a mixing bowl. Next take tablespoons of the mixture and form them into balls, squeezing the mixture together, place them on a flat surface, and flatten them out with the palm of your hand into small cake shapes about 1½ inches in diameter. You should get 16 in all. When all the fish cakes are ready, put them on a plate, cover with plastic wrap, and leave them in the refrigerator for a couple of hours to firm up.

Meanwhile, make the sauce. Place the cucumber, shallots, carrot, chili, ginger, and peanuts in a food processor and pulse till very finely chopped. Transfer the chopped vegetables to a bowl. Next, mix the sugar with the vinegar to dissolve it, then pour it over the vegetables along with the soy sauce and peanut oil. Mix thoroughly.

To cook the fish cakes, heat 2 tablespoons of peanut oil in a skillet, and when it's very hot and beginning to shimmer, fry the cakes for about 1 minute on each side, then drain on crumpled paper towels. Garnish with sprigs of cilantro and serve with the cucumber dipping sauce.

———————— ◊ ————————

Angel Hair Pasta
with Thai Spiced Shrimp

·

SERVES 2 AS A MAIN COURSE OR 4 AS A FIRST COURSE

Angel hair pasta (capellini) is, as the name suggests, the very finest shreds of pasta. This dish, made with jumbo shrimp, is spicy, pungent, and just the thing to make use of some previously prepared Thai Red Curry Paste.

4 tablespoons Thai Red Curry Paste (page 51)	**¾ cup dry white wine**
16 jumbo shrimp, peeled and deveined	**salt and freshly ground black pepper**
¼ cup light olive oil	**6 ozs. angel hair pasta**
5 cloves garlic, chopped	
2 large tomatoes, skinned, deseeded, and chopped	**TO GARNISH:**
grated zest and juice of 1 lime	**3 tablespoons chopped fresh cilantro**
	a few paper-thin slices of fresh lime, cut in half

A couple of hours before you intend to serve the pasta, place the Thai Red Curry Paste in a bowl, add the shrimp, and toss them around so that they get a good coating of sauce. Now cover the bowl with plastic wrap and refrigerate for a couple of hours for the shrimp to soak up the flavor.

When you're ready to start cooking, heat up 2 tablespoons of oil in a skillet and gently cook the garlic for 1 or 2 minutes, or until it's pale gold, then add the chopped tomatoes, lime zest and juice, and wine, and keeping the heat high, let the sauce bubble and reduce for about 8 minutes. After that, add the shrimp and paste to the sauce, and when it's bubbling again, turn the heat down and let it cook gently for another 3 minutes, or until it has reduced and thickened. Then put a lid on the skillet and keep the sauce warm while you deal with the pasta.

For this you need to make sure that you have two plates warming, then bring a large saucepan of salted water up to a fast boil. Push the pasta down into the boiling water and immediately time it for 3 minutes only. As soon as the 3 minutes are up, spoon the pasta (using a spoon and fork, or a proper pasta server) directly onto the plates. Don't worry about the wetness, as this will soon evaporate: if you drain this pasta in the normal way, because it's so fine it sticks together and becomes unmanageable. Now quickly spoon the sauce and shrimp over the pasta, sprinkle on the cilantro, add the lime slices, and serve *presto pronto!*

———— ◊ ————

Thai Salmon Filo Parcels

SERVES 2

For waist watchers and the health-conscious, the growing popularity of filo pastry is, I'm sure, warmly welcomed. But I also suspect we could be in danger of overkill, so I like to use it only where it's really appropriate — like here, where cooking the fish in a parcel really does seal in all those precious salmon juices, and when they mingle with the lime, ginger, and cilantro, the result is marvelous!

1 teaspoon grated fresh ginger	**salt and freshly ground**
grated zest and juice of 1 lime	**black pepper**
1 clove garlic, crushed	
1 tablespoon chopped fresh	**TO GARNISH:**
cilantro	**sprigs of cilantro**
1 scallion, finely chopped	**1 lime, cut into quarters**
¼ stick butter	
4 sheets filo pastry, each about	**You will also need a baking sheet.**
12 × 7 inches	
2 salmon fillets cut from the thicker	
part of the fish, 4 to 5 ozs. each	Preheat the oven to 375°F.

First of all, in a small bowl mix together the ginger, lime zest, garlic, cilantro, and chopped scallions, then stir in the lime juice. Now melt the butter in a small saucepan. Lay 1 sheet of filo pastry out on a flat surface, brush it all over with melted butter, spread another sheet of filo on top, and brush this lightly with melted butter as well.

Position one of the salmon fillets near to one end of the filo, season it, and sprinkle half the lime-and-herb mixture on top. Next, fold the short end of pastry over the salmon, then fold the long sides inward, fold the salmon over twice more, and trim any surplus pastry (it's important not to end up with great wedges of pastry at each end). Wrap the other piece of salmon in exactly the same way, and when you're ready to cook, brush the parcels all over with melted butter, place them on a baking sheet, and bake in the oven for 20 to 25 minutes, or until the pastry is brown and crisp. Serve garnished with sprigs of cilantro and wedges of lime.

◊

Baked Salmon *and* Sorrel Galettes

.

SERVES 6 AS A FIRST COURSE

The sharp, almost lemony flavor of sorrel leaves contrasts beautifully with fresh salmon. If sorrel isn't available, however, young spinach leaves or even outer lettuce leaves can be used instead. The leaves are used to make a kind of casing around the salmon, which looks very pretty.

2 ozs. young sorrel or spinach leaves, washed, stems removed	**4 egg yolks**
6 ozs. fillet of salmon, prepared weight	**TO GARNISH: sprigs of watercress**
1 cup milk	
1 bay leaf	**You will also need 6 ramekins**
1 blade of mace	**(½-cup size) , lightly buttered, and**
salt and freshly ground black pepper	**a baking sheet.**
2 teaspoons chopped fresh tarragon	
⅔ cup heavy cream	Preheat the oven to 325°F.

First, steam the sorrel leaves for 1 minute only, using a basket steamer. Pat them dry and line the ramekins with them. You'll probably find a pastry brush is helpful here to ease the leaves into place. Overlap them so as not to leave any gaps, and allow the tops to hang over the dish edges, as they can be folded in afterward.

Now to deal with the fish: Place it in a saucepan along with the milk, bay leaf, and blade of mace, add some salt and pepper, then bring it to a simmer and simmer for 4 minutes exactly — no more, as it needs to be really moist. Strain the milk into a small bowl, then flake the salmon into large flakes and divide them equally among the ramekins, sprinkling in the chopped tarragon and a little seasoning.

Return the milk to the saucepan, add the cream, and heat gently while you beat the egg yolks in the bowl the milk was in. As soon as the milk mixture barely simmers, pour it over the eggs, mix thoroughly, then pour the whole lot into the ramekins. Fold any overlapping leaves over the mixture, place the ramekins on the baking sheet, and put them on a highish shelf of the oven to bake for 20 to 25 minutes, or until the centers of the galettes are just set and the tops turning brown. Remove them from the oven and leave for 10 to 15 minutes to settle before turning them out onto warmed plates. Garnish with watercress and serve straightaway. These also taste good served with some young salad leaves dressed with Lemon Vinaigrette (page 68).

◊

Chilled Marinated Trout
with Fennel

·

SERVES 2

This makes a very appropriate main course for a warm day. It's a breeze to prepare, and it has the advantage of being cooked and left to marinate, so that when the time comes, you have literally nothing to do but serve it. I particularly like this either with a plain mixed-leaf salad or with a half-quantity of Pesto Rice Salad (page 28).

2 medium-sized bright fresh rainbow trout (about 8 ozs. each)	**1 cup dry white wine**
¾ teaspoon whole black peppercorns	**½ teaspoon fresh oregano**
¾ teaspoon coriander seeds	**1 bulb fennel, trimmed, quartered, and finely sliced (green tops reserved)**
½ teaspoon fennel seeds	
2 tablespoons extra-virgin olive oil	
1 clove garlic, finely chopped	**FOR THE GARNISH:**
1 small onion, finely chopped	**2 scallions, finely chopped**
1 lb. ripe, red tomatoes, skinned and chopped	**2 tablespoons chopped parsley**
1 tablespoon fresh lemon juice	**grated zest of 1 lemon**
1 tablespoon white wine vinegar	**fennel tops**
salt and freshly ground black pepper	

You will also need a 10-inch skillet.

Begin by washing the fish and drying it with paper towels. Then warm the skillet over a gentle heat. Crush the peppercorns, coriander, and fennel seeds in a mortar, put them in the skillet, and let them dry-roast for about 1 minute to draw out the flavors. Next, add the olive oil, garlic, and onion and cook gently for about 5 minutes, or until the onion is pale gold.

Then add the tomatoes, lemon juice, wine vinegar, and white wine, stir, and when it begins to bubble, season with salt and pepper and add the oregano. Now add the sliced fennel to the pan, followed by the trout, which should be basted with the juices. Put a timer on and give the whole thing 10 minutes' gentle simmering. After that use a spatula and fork to turn each fish over carefully onto its other side — don't prod it or anything like that or the flesh will break. Then give it another 10 minutes' cooking on the other side.

Gently remove the trout to a shallow platter, spoon the sauce all over, let cool, cover with plastic wrap, and leave them in a cool place. If you want to make this dish the day before, that's okay provided you keep it refrigerated and remove it an hour before serving. Either way, sprinkle each trout with the garnish (made by simply combining all the garnish ingredients together) before taking them to the table.

NOTE: If the weather's chilly, this dish is excellent served warm with tiny new potatoes and a leafy salad.

◇

Californian Broiled Fish

.

SERVES 2

If you have a jar of the lovely Quick Cilantro and Lime Tartar Sauce (see next recipe), a wonderful way to use it is to spread it over some fish fillets, then sprinkle with cheese and breadcrumbs and pop them under a preheated broiler. You'll have one of the fastest and most delectable suppers imaginable.

2 fish fillets (cod, hake, whiting, sole — anything you like), weighing about 7 ozs. each

salt and freshly ground black pepper

2 tablespoons Quick Cilantro and Lime Tartar Sauce (page 59)

2 tablespoons fresh white or whole-wheat breadcrumbs

3 tablespoons grated Cheddar

1 tablespoon chopped fresh cilantro

pinch of cayenne pepper

grated zest of ½ lime

1 tablespoon butter

You will also need a broiler pan lined with foil smeared with a trace of butter.

Preheat the broiler to its highest setting.

Begin by wiping the fish fillets with paper towels to get them as dry as possible. Then place them in the foil-lined broiler pan. Season with salt and pepper, and spread the tartar sauce all over the surface of the fish. Now mix the bread-crumbs, cheese, cilantro, cayenne, and lime zest in a bowl and sprinkle over the fish as evenly as possible. Dot with a little butter. Place the pan as far from the heat as possible and broil the fish for 10–15 minutes, depending on its thickness — it should be just cooked through and the top should be crispy and golden. Serve with tiny new potatoes tossed in chives and lemon juice, and a plain lettuce salad.

———— ◊ ————

Quick Cilantro *and* Lime Tartar Sauce

·

SERVES 4

When someone brought me back a menu from the famous Bel Air Hotel in Los Angeles and I saw this sauce, I couldn't wait to try it. I love the way American chefs are un-afraid to introduce Eastern ingredients into Western recipes — in this case a classic tartar sauce, normally made with lemon juice and parsley, is transformed by the more Asian flavors of lime juice and cilantro. Brilliant.

1 large egg	**1 tablespoon fresh lime juice**
½ teaspoon salt	**1½ tablespoons small capers, drained**
freshly ground black pepper	
1 small clove garlic, peeled	**3 large or 4 small cornichons, finely chopped**
½ teaspoon mustard power	
¾ cup light olive oil	**2 tablespoons chopped fresh cilantro**

Tartar sauce has a mayonnaise base, which in this case is made by the quick method — that is, using a whole egg and a food processor or blender. Break the egg into the bowl of the processor and add salt, pepper, garlic, and mustard. Switch on the motor and, through the feed tube, add the oil in a thin, steady trickle, pouring it as slowly as you can (which even then will take only about 2 minutes). When the oil is in and the sauce has thickened, transfer the mayonnaise to a bowl using a rubber spatula, then add all the other ingredients. Taste to check the seasoning before serving, and since this is a mayonnaise-based sauce, be sure to keep it cool and refrigerated until immediately before serving. This sauce will keep in a screw-top jar in the refrigerator for up to a week. Serve with any plain grilled fish or with fish cakes.

◊

CHAPTER FOUR

THE VEGETABLES
of
SPRING *and*
SUMMER

————————— ◇ —————————

During the summer in which I was preparing this book, a discon-
certing thing happened. Included in my once-a-week supermarket
shopping was a bag containing fresh young peas in the pod; the
young woman at the checkout counter (who looked all of sixteen)
puzzled over the bag, trying, I thought, to find the price. But then she looked up
and said, "Can you tell me what these are, please?" How sad that any young
person would not have had the pleasure of bursting open moist young pods
and munching on the odd raw tender pea — for me it was always one of the
lazy pleasures of summer, sitting in the garden shelling peas. What has happened, of course, is that the frozen pea industry has become huge, and only
those peas too old for freezing now find their way into the stores as "fresh,"
which, alas, has made people *think* they don't like fresh peas.

This chapter does not contain many recipes as such, but that is because of
my conviction that young vegetables do not need recipes: it would be almost
criminal to mask their flavor in any way. Later on in summer, though, they
might need a little help from the cook, and that is why the idea of oven-roasting
vegetables has fired my imagination. There are a number of suggestions on this
way of cooking in the book, and I can assure you that it adds a whole new dimension to the vegetables, and as a bonus, they require very little attention
while cooking.

————————————————————

Warm Potato Salad
with Lemon *and* Chive Vinaigrette

·

SERVES 4 TO 6

This recipe can be served warm, as an accompanying vegetable, or cold as part of a group of salads — in which case you still need to pour on the dressing while the potatoes are warm.

2 lbs. new potatoes (as small as possible), skins on, washed	grated zest of 1 lemon
2 sprigs of fresh mint	⅓ cup extra-virgin olive oil
salt	1 heaping teaspoon grain mustard
	freshly ground black pepper
FOR THE LEMON AND CHIVE VINAIGRETTE:	**TO GARNISH:**
1 clove garlic	2 tablespoons snipped fresh chives
1 teaspoon coarse salt	6 scallions, trimmed and chopped small
⅓ cup fresh lemon juice	

First of all, place the potatoes in a saucepan with enough boiling water just to cover them, add the mint and some salt, and simmer for about 15 to 20 minutes, or until tender.

Meanwhile, make the vinaigrette. Using a mortar and pestle, crush the garlic and salt together to a paste, then gradually mix in all the other vinaigrette ingredients.

When the potatoes are cooked, drain them in a colander and transfer them to a serving bowl. Pour on the vinaigrette dressing while they are still hot and toss them around in the dressing to get a good coating. Finally, scatter in the chopped chives and scallions and serve.

———————— ◇ ————————

Oven-Roasted Ratatouille

SERVES 4

*I*f *you like ratatouille, once you've tried it roasted like this you'll never go back to the traditional method. Not only do the vegetables retain their shape and identity, but they also take on a lovely toasted flavor.*

2 medium-sized zucchini	**2 fat cloves garlic, finely chopped**
1 small eggplant	**1 handful fresh basil leaves**
salt and freshly ground black pepper	**¼ cup olive oil**
1 lb. cherry tomatoes, skinned	
1 small red bell pepper, deseeded and cut into 1-inch squares	**You will also need a large shallow roasting pan, about 16 × 12 inches.**
1 small yellow bell pepper, deseeded and cut into 1-inch squares	
1 medium-sized onion, peeled and chopped into 1-inch squares	Preheat the oven to its highest setting.

Prepare the zucchini and eggplant ahead of time by cutting them into 1-inch dice, leaving their skins on. Now sprinkle with 2 teaspoons salt, then pack them into a colander with a plate on top and a heavy weight on top of that. Leave them like this for an hour, so that the bitter juices can drain out. After that, squeeze out any juices that are left and dry the vegetables thoroughly with paper towels.

Arrange the tomatoes, zucchini, eggplant, peppers, and onion in a roasting pan and sprinkle the garlic over them. Tear up the basil leaves roughly and mix with the olive oil. Drizzle the oil over the vegetables, making sure that each one has a good coating, and season with salt and pepper. Roast on the highest shelf of the oven for 30 to 40 minutes, or until the vegetables are roasted and tinged brown at the edges. Remove from the oven, using an oven mitt, as the pan will be very hot, and serve straightaway.

———————— ◊ ————————

Sliced Potatoes Baked *with* Tomatoes *and* Basil

·

SERVES 4 TO 6

Just when the new potatoes are getting too big to be really new, the red, ripe tomatoes of summer are at their best and the basil leaves are large and opulent. This dish is a wonderful way to combine all three, and I love to serve this with Chicken with Sherry Vinegar and Tarragon Sauce (page 118).

1 lb. red, ripe tomatoes
2 lbs. potatoes, skins on
1 fat clove garlic, finely chopped
1 onion, finely chopped
salt and freshly ground black pepper
½ cup fresh basil leaves
1 tablespoon extra-virgin olive oil

You will also need a round or oval gratin dish about 9 inches wide, lightly oiled.

Preheat the oven to 375°F.

First of all, pour boiling water over the tomatoes, leave them for 1 minute, then drain them and slip the skins off, protecting your hands with a cloth as necessary. Chop the flesh quite small. Then slice the potatoes thinly. Now, in a gratin dish, arrange a layer of sliced potato, a little chopped garlic and onion, and some seasoning, followed by some chopped tomato, some more seasoning, and a few torn basil leaves. Repeat all this until you have incorporated all the ingredients, then drizzle a little oil over the surface and bake in the oven for about 1 hour, or until the potatoes are tender.

◇

Roasted Fennel Niçoise

·

SERVES 4 AS A FIRST COURSE

The slight aniseed flavor of fennel holds its own perfectly with the gutsy provençale flavors of anchovies, olives, and tomatoes. This is a lovely dish to serve warm with fish, meat, or poultry, on its own as a first course, or even cold as a salad for a buffet lunch.

3 medium bulbs fennel
1 tablespoon olive oil

FOR THE DRESSING:

1 clove garlic
1 teaspoon coarse salt
2 tablespoons fresh lemon juice
⅓ cup extra-virgin olive oil
2 large beefsteak tomatoes, skinned, deseeded, and finely chopped
12 black olives, pitted and chopped
1 shallot, finely chopped

4 anchovy fillets, drained and chopped
freshly ground black pepper

TO GARNISH:
a few fresh basil leaves and fennel fronds

You will also need a shallow baking sheet.

Preheat the oven to 375°F.

Begin by preparing the fennel: First trim off any green fronds and reserve them for the garnish. Now lay the fennel bulbs flat on a board and trim off the root base, then cut the stalk ends away by making two diagonal cuts so that the bulbs look pointed at the top. Cut each bulb into quarters, then cut away the center stalky parts and slice the quarters into eighths, being careful to leave the layers attached to the root ends.

Place the fennel in a saucepan, cover with boiling water, season with some salt, and simmer for just 5 minutes, no longer. Then drain the fennel in a colander so it can dry off a little. Put 1 tablespoon olive oil in a saucer and use it to brush first the baking sheet and then each piece of fennel before arranging them on the sheet. Roast the fennel on a high shelf in the oven for 30 minutes, or until it is nicely tinged with brown at the edges and is cooked through but still retains some bite.

While the fennel is roasting, make up the dressing. Using a mortar and pestle, crush the garlic to a paste together with 1 teaspoon of salt, then beat in the lemon juice and oil, and when it has amalgamated, combine it with the rest of the dressing ingredients.

When the fennel's ready, transfer it to a shallow serving bowl and pour the dressing over it while it is still warm. Taste to check the seasoning — it will need some freshly ground pepper — and scatter with the chopped fennel fronds and some torn basil leaves just before serving.

———————— ◊ ————————

Compote of Garlic *and*
Sweet Bell Peppers

·

SERVES 6 TO 8

This is a really robust, deliciously full-bodied combination that goes well with spicy sausages or barbecued meats. Serve as part of a buffet and just see how many people go back for seconds!

Begin by washing, halving, and deseeding the peppers. Cut the halves into quarters and the quarters into ¼-inch-thick strips. Then place a large saucepan

2 lbs. bell peppers (red, yellow, and orange — but not green)	**10 cloves garlic, finely chopped**
3 teaspoons cumin seeds, lightly crushed	**2 teaspoons mild chili powder**
	5 tablespoons tomato paste
¼ cup olive oil	**salt**

over medium heat, add the crushed cumin seeds, and toss them around in the heat to draw out their flavor. Add the oil and let it gently heat for a minute. Now stir in the sliced peppers, garlic, and chili powder. Cook for 1 minute, stirring so that the ingredients are thoroughly mixed, cover the pan, and continue to cook over a low heat for a further 30 to 40 minutes, or until the pepper strips are quite soft.

Now uncover the pan, increase the heat to medium, and stir in the tomato paste. Continue to cook (uncovered) until no free liquid remains — this takes about 15 minutes. Finally, taste and add salt and some more tomato paste if the mixture seems to need a little more body and sweetness. Serve the compote warm, or if you want to serve it as part of a buffet, it's fine served cool (but not chilled).

———————— ◊ ————————

Baby Summer Vegetables *with* Lemon Vinaigrette

·

SERVES 6 TO 8

This is another versatile recipe that can be served either warm as a vegetable or cold as a salad — a truly beautiful combination of those first, young, tender vegetables of early summer.

12 ozs. fava beans — prepared weight (about 4 lbs. in the shell)	**grated zest of 1 lemon**
8 ozs. fresh tiny baby carrots	**2 tablespoons white wine vinegar**
10 pearl onions, the smallest you can find	**⅔ cup light olive oil**
8 ozs. fresh garden peas — prepared weight (1½ lbs. in the shell)	**2 teaspoons mustard powder**
	TO GARNISH:
FOR THE LEMON VINAIGRETTE:	**1 tablespoon chopped fresh herbs (mint and chives)**
¼ cup fresh lemon juice	**You will also need a steamer.**

To get the very best color and texture (and if you have the patience), it's best to fillet the fava beans. So after shelling, pour boiling water over them, and when the water has cooled sufficiently, simply slip off the outer skin, which will reveal the beautiful vivid green inner bean in two halves.

Next, put the carrots in a steamer fitted over a pan of simmering water, steam them for 4 minutes precisely, then add the pearl onions and the peas and continue to steam for a further 3 to 4 minutes.

Meanwhile, make up the vinaigrette dressing by placing all the ingredients together in a screw-top jar, putting on the lid, and shaking vigorously to combine everything.

When the vegetables are tender but still retain their bite, remove the steamer, throw out the water from the pan, and put the fava beans in the pan along with the rest of the vegetables and the dressing. Toss everything around over a gentle heat for about 1 minute. Then transfer it all to a warmed platter, sprinkle the herbs over the vegetables as a garnish, and serve.

————————— ◊ —————————

Baby Summer Vegetables with Lemon Vinaigrette

Oven-Roasted Potatoes *with* Garlic *and* Rosemary

·

SERVES 4 TO 6

I*n keeping with the principle that outdoor eating needs to be gutsy, these little potatoes are just that. They're easy too — they don't need any attention; you just leave them in the oven till you're ready to serve.*

3 tablespoons olive oil
2 lbs. large new potatoes, skins on
1 or 2 cloves garlic, finely chopped
2 tablespoons fresh rosemary leaves, finely chopped
salt and freshly ground black pepper

You will also need a heavy, shallow roasting pan measuring about 16 × 12 inches.

Preheat the oven to 425°F.

Begin by measuring the oil into the roasting pan, then pop it into the oven to heat it through. Wash the potatoes, but don't scrape the skins off, then cut them into cubes of roughly ½ inch. Place them in a clean dish towel and dry them as thoroughly as you can, then transfer them to a large plate.

Remove the pan from the oven, place it over direct heat — the oil needs to be very hot — then carefully slide the potatoes straight into the hot oil. Turn them around to get a good coating of oil, sprinkling in the garlic and rosemary as you go. Return the pan to the oven and roast for 30 to 40 minutes, or until the potatoes are golden brown and crisp. Season with salt and pepper before serving.

———— ◊ ————

Red-Coated Zucchini

SERVES 2 TO 4

T*he zucchini in our garden proliferate so quickly that I'm always looking for new ways of serving them. This is one of the most delicious and speediest.*

2 tablespoons olive oil	1 fat clove garlic, crushed
1 small onion, finely chopped	1½ heaping teaspoons fresh oregano
12 ozs. young zucchini	salt and freshly ground black
12 ozs. red, ripe tomatoes	pepper

You will need your largest, widest skillet for this. Begin by heating 1 tablespoon of oil in the pan and frying the onion gently for 5 minutes. Meanwhile, wipe the zucchini, trim off the ends, and cut them into slices about ¼ inch thick. Now remove the onion to a plate. Turn up the heat, add the rest of the oil, and when it's really hot, add the zucchini slices to the pan, spreading them out in one layer. Fry them to color lightly on both sides.

While that's happening, pour boiling water over the tomatoes, and after 1 minute, slip the skins off and roughly chop the flesh. When the zucchini are a nice golden color, return the onion to the pan and add the chopped tomatoes. Sprinkle in the crushed garlic, the oregano, and some seasoning. Simmer gently, stirring every now and then, for about 10 minutes, or until the tomato pulp has reduced and thickened and completely coats the zucchini.

◇

CHAPTER FIVE

BARBECUE *and* OUTDOOR FOOD

———— ◇ ————

Barbecuing has become a way of life. It's not just for parties but for everyday cooking. The wonderful thing about barbecuing is that in a way this type of cooking doesn't need recipes: plain steaks, sausages, and chops — anything with a gutsy flavor — all taste better cooked out of doors on charcoal. So does fresh fish.

The whole point of outdoor eating and the whole point of the recipes in this chapter is that they have lots of character and flavor. What pleases me most is that at last I've even found a barbecue recipe for vegetarians (page 82), who are the ones who so often feel left out of this type of meal.

————

Preceding pages from left to right: Crisp salad with American Blue Cheese Dressing (page 34); All-American Half-Pounders (page 78), Oven-Roasted Potatoes with Garlic and Rosemary (page 70).

A Mixed Grill
with Apricot Barbecue Glaze

·

SERVES 6

This is a sauce that's suitable for all meats — lamb chops, pork ribs, or chicken drumsticks. The quantity is enough to glaze six of each, which makes a nice mixture of meats to serve to six people. One important point is that drumsticks need prebaking in a preheated oven at 350°F for 15 minutes just before glazing and barbecuing.

FOR THE APRICOT BARBECUE GLAZE:	2 tablespoons tomato paste
2 large apricots	1 clove garlic
3 tablespoons dark brown sugar	freshly ground black pepper
¼ cup Worcestershire sauce	
¼ cup light soy sauce	FOR THE MEATS:
1 tablespoon grated fresh ginger	6 rib lamb chops
1½ teaspoons ginger powder	6 pork ribs
a few drops of Tabasco	6 small to medium-sized chicken drumsticks

Begin by placing the apricots in a small saucepan with enough water to cover them, then bring them up to a simmer and simmer for 2 minutes. Drain off the water, and as soon as they are cool enough to handle, slip off the skins. Then halve and pit them and place the flesh in a blender or food processor together with all the other glaze ingredients. Purée it all together and the sauce is ready.

All you need to do now is arrange the lamb and pork in a shallow dish, pour the glaze over them — turning the pieces of meat so that each one gets a good coating — then cover and leave in a cool place until you're ready to cook.

When you light the charcoal, precook the chicken drumsticks as directed above, then, when your charcoal is at the right heat, brush the drumsticks with the glaze and cook for about 5 minutes on each side about 3 inches from the coals. The ribs and chops will need about 6 minutes on each side, but take the lamb off before 12 minutes if you like it very rare.

What I like to do sometimes is to make a little extra sauce by scraping any glaze that's left in the dish into a small saucepan, adding a glass of white wine, and bringing it all to a simmer. Serve the barbecued glazed meats with Oven-Roasted Potatoes with Garlic and Rosemary (page 70), a crisp salad, and some very robust red wine!

◊

Spiced Lamb *and* Cashew Kebabs

.

SERVES 4

Not long ago I was fortunate enough to have a holiday in Hong Kong and visited a restaurant at Repulse Bay called Spices. I was so taken by the spicy kebabs I had there that on my return home I immediately tried to make them — and I think this is fairly close to the original!

1 teaspoon cumin seeds
1 teaspoon coriander seeds
12 ozs. shoulder of lamb, boned
(80 percent lean meat, as some
fat is important to keep it juicy)
1 small onion, quartered
1 clove garlic
⅓ cup chopped fresh cilantro leaves

juice of ½ lime
1 cup roasted and salted
cashew nuts
1 fresh green chili, deseeded
salt and freshly ground black pepper
a little peanut oil

You will also need 4 long, flat metal skewers.

First of all, you need to roast the cumin and coriander seeds. To do this, place them in a small skillet or saucepan over medium heat and stir and toss them around for about 1 to 2 minutes, or until they begin to look toasted and start to "jump" in the pan. Transfer them to a mortar and crush them with a pestle to a powder.

To make the kebabs, you need to cut the meat into chunks and place it in a food processor, along with the onion, garlic, fresh cilantro leaves, lime juice, cashews, chili, spices, and seasoning. Switch the motor on and off and pulse until you have ground everything together but it still has some identity — it needs to end up like very coarse sausage meat. Now take about a tablespoon of the mixture and roll it on a flat surface into a sausage shape, squeezing it firmly together. Pat and square off the ends to give it a nice shape. Repeat until you have used all the mixture: you should aim to finish up with twelve. Thread these onto skewers, three on each. Cover them with plastic wrap and refrigerate until needed. (It's important to leave them for at least 2 hours anyway to firm up.)

Brush the kebabs with oil and broil for about 5 minutes on each side — either indoors, 2 inches from the broiler, or outside over hot charcoal. Serve with Sweet Bell Pepper and Cilantro Relish (page 77) and some Spiced Rice Pilaf (page 114).

———————— ◊ ————————

Sweet Bell Pepper *and* Cilantro Relish

·

SERVES 4

This is made in moments if you have a food processor, and you won't believe how good it tastes. Serve it with Spiced Lamb and Cashew Kebabs (see previous recipe) or with plain grilled or barbecued meats.

1 fresh green chili	⅓ cup fresh lime juice
1 medium-sized red bell pepper	2 large tomatoes, skinned, deseeded, and chopped
1 small red onion	
½ cup chopped fresh cilantro	salt and freshly ground black pepper

Just place all the ingredients in a food processor and switch on to blend evenly to the stage where it looks as though everything is chopped minutely small but hasn't lost its identity. Set aside (covered) in a cool place and stir well before serving.

———————— ◊ ————————

All-American Half-Pounders

SERVES 4

There are several kinds of hamburgers, ranging from those that come frozen or are served up in fast-food chains to the slightly more classy supermarket varieties. The real thing consists of good steak chopped and tenderized, formed into burgers, and grilled on charcoal. The degree of thickness in a hamburger is paramount, since a thick burger ensures a crisp, charred outside and a juicy, rare, medium-rare, or whatever-you-like inside. I find that 4 ounces of meat is perfect if it is going to be served in a bun, but 8 ounces is best for a more sophisticated adult version. Personally, I prefer it to eating a plain grilled steak.

2 lbs. best ground round or sirloin if you're feeling flush, otherwise ground chuck — either way, make sure that it contains 20 percent fat	**salt and freshly ground black pepper** **a little oil**

If you're on a diet, don't eat a hamburger: it really is vital that it contain 20 percent fat, as this is what keeps the meat moist while cooking. If you're using chuck steak, trim off any gristle and sinewy bits but hang on to the fat. Cut the meat into chunks, put it into a food processor, and blend until it looks like fine minced beef; however, don't overdo the processing, because if the meat becomes too fine, the burger will have a bouncy texture!

Place the meat in a bowl and season with freshly ground pepper, but don't add salt till after the cooking because it draws out the juices. Now form the mixture into four rounds, pressing each one firmly together (it won't need egg or anything else to keep it together if you press firmly enough). Place the burgers on a plate, cover with plastic wrap, and leave in the refrigerator until you're ready to cook them.

When the barbecue is good and hot, brush the grill with a little oil to prevent the meat from sticking to it, and give the burgers a light coating of oil too. Broil them for 4 to 6 minutes on each side, depending on how you like them. The same timing also applies to an oven broiler turned to its highest setting.

Serve the half-pounders with Mexican Tomato Salsa (page 79), Oven-Roasted Potatoes with Garlic and Rosemary (page 70), or, if you like, a salad with Blue Cheese Dressing (page 34).

—————————— ◊ ——————————

Mexican Tomato Salsa

.

SERVES 4

*S*alsa has the advantage of being a salad, a sauce, and a relish all in one. There's no fat or sugar in it, and the flavor's wonderful. The small, squat, green chilies are not too hot, so if you'd like a little more kick to this, you can add a few drops of Tabasco.

4 large, firm tomatoes	**⅓ cup chopped fresh cilantro**
1 fresh green chili (the fat, squat	**juice of 1 lime**
variety that isn't too fiery)	**salt and freshly ground black**
½ medium red onion, finely chopped	**pepper**

Place the tomatoes in a bowl, pour boiling water over them, then after 1 minute drain them and slip off the skins, protecting your hands with a cloth if you need to. Cut each tomato in half and hold each half in the palm of your hand (cut side up), then turn your hand over and squeeze gently until the seeds come out — it's best to do this over a plate or bowl to catch the seeds!

Now, using a sharp knife, chop the tomatoes into approximately ¼-inch dice straight into a serving bowl. Next, destem the chili, cut it in half, remove the seeds, and chop the flesh very finely before adding it to the tomatoes. Add the chopped onion, cilantro, and lime juice and season with salt and pepper. Give everything a thorough mixing, then cover and set aside for about an hour before serving.

◊

Barbecued Sardines *with* Summer Herb Sauce

.

SERVES 4

*I*t's not that easy to find fresh sardines, but if you can get hold of them, you'll find that they have a very evocative flavor and aroma that perfectly suit eating out of doors. This is a recipe that can easily be prepared well ahead of time, and if the coals on the barbecue are good and hot, the fish are cooked in moments. If sorrel is unavailable, use young spinach leaves mixed with some grated zest of lemon — about 1 tablespoon — for the stuffing.

2 lbs. fresh sardines (about 12)	1½ tablespoons chopped fresh basil
6 ozs. fresh sorrel leaves (stems removed), washed and dried	1½ tablespoons chopped flat-leaf parsley or chervil
salt and freshly ground black pepper	3 shallots, finely chopped
about 2 tablespoons olive oil	1 large clove garlic, finely chopped
	3 tablespoons cider vinegar
FOR THE SAUCE:	2 teaspoons balsamic vinegar
1½ tablespoons snipped fresh chives	salt and freshly ground black
1 tablespoon chopped fresh tarragon	pepper

First, prepare the sardines: Use a small pair of scissors to cut open the bellies and remove the innards. Then wipe them inside and out with damp paper towels and arrange them on a plate. Next, chop the sorrel leaves fairly finely, then season them and stuff three-quarters of them inside the bellies of the fish. Sprinkle the oil over the fish and rub it in so that they all get a good coating.

Now prepare the sauce: Place the remaining sorrel leaves, along with the other herbs, the shallots, and the garlic, in a pitcher or serving bowl and add 5 tablespoons boiling water, followed by the vinegars. Stir well and season with salt and pepper.

The sardines will need very little time to cook — just 2 minutes on each side. Serve the sauce handed around separately. These are also very good served with Oven-Roasted Potatoes with Garlic and Rosemary (page 70) and Roasted Fennel Niçoise (page 66).

NOTE: If it rains, the sardines will cook perfectly well under a broiler or on a ridged grill pan.

———————— ◊ ————————

Barbecued Sardines with Summer Herb Sauce

Marinated Halloumi Cheese Kebabs *with* Herbs

·

SERVES 2

Vegetarians often tend to feel deprived when invited to barbecues, so I spent an entire day last summer finding something that broils well on charcoal and has all the fun and flavor — but without meat. This was the one that filled the bill perfectly.

1 medium-sized bell pepper (any color)	**parsley (or similar combination of**
1 medium-sized red onion	**whatever herbs are available)**
12 ozs. halloumi cheese (see Note), cut	**1 fat clove garlic**
into 1-inch cubes	**¼ cup extra-virgin olive oil**
4 medium-sized mushrooms	**juice of 1 lime**
	freshly ground black pepper
FOR THE MARINADE:	
1 teaspoon each of chopped fresh	**You will also need 2 flat metal skewers**
thyme, oregano, rosemary, mint, and	**(12 inches long).**

Begin by cutting the pepper and onion into even-sized pieces about 1 inch square, to match the size of the cubes of cheese. Then chop the herbs and garlic quite finely and combine them with the oil, lime juice, and some freshly ground pepper. Now place the cheese, onion, pepper, and mushrooms in a large, roomy bowl and pour the marinade over them, mixing very thoroughly. Cover and refrigerate for 24 hours, and try to give them a stir-around every now and then.

When you're ready to barbecue the kebabs, take the two skewers and thread a mushroom on first (pushing it right down), followed by a piece of onion, a piece of pepper, and a cube of cheese. Repeat this with more onion, pepper, and cheese, finishing with a mushroom at the end. Place the kebabs over the hot coals, turning frequently till they are tinged brown at the edges — about 10 minutes. Brush on any leftover marinade juices as you turn them. Serve with Mexican Tomato Salsa (page 79) and Oven-Roasted Potatoes with Garlic and Rosemary (page 70).

NOTE: Halloumi cheese is available from Lebanese, Greek, and Arabic food stores.

———————— ◊ ————————

Grilled Corn

·

SERVES 4

I think this is the nicest way to eat corn. If you don't have a barbecue going, you can cook the corn under a preheated oven broiler.

4 ears of corn	salt and freshly ground black pepper
2 tablespoons olive oil	

Remove the husks and silk from the corn, then brush the kernels all over with the oil, seasoning them liberally with salt and pepper as you go. Place the ears of corn on a grill over hot coals and watch them carefully, turning them around with tongs so that all the kernels get toasted to a golden-brown color. The whole process will take about 5 to 10 minutes, depending on how far the corn is from the heat. Test each one with a skewer to check that it is tender.

◊

Crunchy Peanut-Coated Drumsticks

SERVES 6

*Y*es, it's really true. Even if you don't like peanuts in the "normal" way, you'll enjoy them used as a coating with a slightly Asian flavor — I've tested this on peanut haters! It is perfect picnic food for both children and adults, but remember to start these off at least eight hours ahead.

12 chicken drumsticks, skin removed	**pinch of cayenne pepper**
5 tablespoons peanut oil	**2 eggs, beaten**
2 tablespoons fresh lemon juice	**¼ cup milk**
1 cup flour	
2 tablespoons medium curry powder	**You will also need a very shallow**
salt and freshly ground black pepper	**baking pan, about 12 × 10 inches,**
1½ cups salted peanuts	**large enough to hold the chicken in**
2 tablespoons fresh cilantro leaves	**one layer.**

First of all, lay the drumsticks in a dish, mix 2 tablespoons of the oil and the lemon juice together, and pour this over the chicken. Then leave the drumsticks to marinate overnight or for at least 8 hours, turning them over once or twice during this period. To make the coating, mix the flour, curry powder, and seasoning together in another shallow dish. When you are ready to cook, toss the drumsticks in the flour mixture, a few at a time. When they are well coated on all sides, tap off the surplus flour and lay them on a plate (reserve any unused flour). Preheat the oven to 425°F.

Now place the nuts, the cilantro leaves, half of the reserved flour, and the cayenne in a food processor and blend. When the mixture is chopped minutely small, transfer it to a plate. After that, beat the eggs and milk together in a bowl. Then take each drumstick and dip it once more first into the remaining seasoned flour, next into the egg mixture, and finally into the peanut mixture. Return the coated drumsticks to their plate and keep cool till needed.

Place the baking pan containing the remaining oil in the oven to preheat, then add the drumsticks to the hot oil (not allowing them to touch one another), baste well, and bake on a high shelf for 15 minutes. Turn the drumsticks over, give them another 15 minutes, then pour off the oil and give them 5 more minutes to get really crisp. Drain on paper towels, and when they are cold, wrap them individually in foil for transportation.

◇

Oven-Baked Chicken *with* Garlic *and* Parmigiano

·

SERVES 4

This is excellent picnic food. Small chicken pieces are so easy to transport and have the advantage of being easy to eat without knives and forks when you get there.

1 chicken (3½ lbs.), cut into 8 pieces, or a mixture of 8 thighs and legs	1 cup fresh breadcrumbs
4 large cloves garlic	½ cup grated Parmigiano-Reggiano
coarse salt and freshly ground black pepper	⅓ cup finely chopped parsley
3 large eggs	You will also need a shallow roasting pan large enough to hold the chicken in one layer.
½ stick butter	
⅓ cup olive oil	

First of all, arrange the chicken pieces in a shallow dish large enough to hold them in a single layer. Place the garlic cloves in a mortar with 1½ teaspoons coarse salt and crush the garlic to a purée. Now add this to the eggs, season with some pepper, and beat well with a fork before pouring the whole lot over the chicken. Cover the dish with plastic wrap and refrigerate for at least 4 hours, turning the chicken pieces over halfway through.

Preheat the oven to 350°F and pop in the shallow roasting pan containing the butter and oil to preheat. Meanwhile, combine the breadcrumbs with the Parmigiano, the parsley, and a little salt and pepper together on a plate, and spread out some paper towels on a flat surface. Remove the chicken from the refrigerator. Take one piece at a time and carefully sit it in the crumb mixture, patting and coating it all over with crumbs (trying not to disturb the egg and garlic already clinging to it). Then lay each piece as it's coated on the paper towels. Next, remove the pan with the now-hot fat in it from the oven and add the chicken pieces. Baste them well and bake on a high shelf for 20 minutes. Then turn the chicken pieces over and give them another 20 minutes before finally pouring off the excess fat from the pan and giving them another 5 minutes.

Drain the chicken on more paper towels, leave to cool, and wrap the pieces individually in foil for transportation.

NOTE: This is also excellent served hot at home with some sliced, lightly sautéed bananas as a garnish.

———————— ◊ ————————

Homemade Lemonade

.

MAKES 3¾ PINTS

*T*here really isn't anything quite like it. There are a million and one commercial versions, but nothing can compare with the flavor of fresh lemons made into lemonade.

6 large lemons	**⅔ cup sugar**

First, scrub the lemons in warm water, then thinly pare the colored outer zest from 3 of them, using a potato peeler or zester. Using a sharp knife, pare away any white pith from the strips of zest — this is important, to keep the lemonade from tasting bitter. Now put the zest in a large bowl and add the squeezed juice of all the lemons (don't bother to strain the juice at this stage) and the sugar.

Next, pour in 6½ cups of boiling water, then stir well, cover, and leave overnight in a cool place. Next day, stir again and taste to check the sweetness, adding a little more sugar if it needs it. Strain through a fairly coarse sieve, as it's nice if some of the lemon remains. Pour the lemonade into bottles, using sterilized corks, then chill thoroughly. Serve the lemonade either straight or diluted with soda water, with lots of ice.

NOTE: To make lemon barley water, proceed as above, but in addition take ¾ cup of pearl barley and rinse thoroughly under a cold tap. Place it in a saucepan and cover with 2 inches of cold water. Bring it to a boil and simmer for 3 to 4 minutes. After that, drain it through a sieve and then rinse and drain again before combining it with the lemon juice, zest, sugar, and boiling water. Leave in a cool place for 24 hours. Then strain and bottle as above.

———————— ◊ ————————

Pineapple Cooler

·

SERVES 4 TO 6

Thistle is an extraordinary drink. It sounds so unlikely, but it really does taste good — not like pineapple but more like cider. It's very refreshing on a hot summer's day, and it's great fun to make in that it uses only the skin of the pineapple, which is normally thrown away — so there's nothing to lose!

the rind of 1 ripe medium pineapple, well rinsed	ice
¼ cup superfine sugar	sprigs of fresh mint

First of all, cut the stalky top and the base off the pineapple and discard them. Stand the pineapple upright on its base, and using a sharp knife, cut away the skin in long strips, working your way all around the fruit. Reserve the fruit itself for a dessert.

Now get to work with a sharp knife, chopping the skin into small pieces about 1 inch square. Pile them all into a bowl, pour 4 cups cold water over them, then cover the bowl with a cloth and leave at room temperature for 3 to 4 days, or until the mixture is bubbly and fermenting. Strain it into a pitcher, add sugar to taste, and serve with lots of ice and sprigs of mint.

———— ◊ ————

Debbie Owen's
Iced Tea

.

SERVES 6 TO 8

The British may be experts at making and serving tea, but when it comes to iced tea, I'm the first to admit the Americans have the edge. I first tasted this version at my friends', the Owens', Fourth of July party several years ago and have been addicted to it ever since.

6 English Breakfast tea bags	**1 ¼ cups orange juice, chilled**
2 tablespoons superfine sugar	**juice of ½ lime**
about 12 sprigs of fresh mint	**½ orange, sliced**
lots of ice	**½ lemon, sliced**

Make up some very strong tea in a large teapot using the tea bags and 5 cups boiling water. Then add the sugar and 6 sprigs of mint to the teapot. Allow the tea to infuse for 15 to 20 minutes, then remove the tea bags, and when the tea is absolutely cooled, remove the mint from the teapot. After that, put lots of ice into a glass pitcher and pour in the cooled tea, followed by the orange and lime juices and the remaining sprigs of mint. Finally, add the orange and lemon slices, stir thoroughly, and serve in glasses with more ice.

———————— ◊ ————————

CHAPTER SIX

A VEGETARIAN SUMMER

———— ◇ ————

T ime was when a vegetarian was just that: someone who ate no meat or fish but only vegetable products. Nowadays, there are many shades of opinion and many layers of being a non–meat eater. Throughout this book — not just in this chapter — I have included all kinds of recipes that do not contain meat, but there are also quite a number for those who are pure vegetarians. Hence this particular section, though by inclination I would prefer not to isolate it as something apart, since I believe vegetarian cooking now belongs in the mainstream of cookery and should not be viewed as something special.

Although I eat meat and fish, I do believe that we all owe much to the vegetarian movement — not least for persuading us to make better use of a wider range of vegetables, grains, and so on. The challenge now is to make vegetarian recipes even more imaginative.

————————————

Rigatoni *and* Asparagus *au* Gratin

·

SERVES 2

*T*his is an excellent way to turn some asparagus stalks into a substantial supper dish for two people.

1¼ cups whole milk	1 lb. ripe, red tomatoes, skinned and chopped
3 tablespoons flour	
1½ tablespoons butter	5 ozs. rigatoni
salt and freshly ground black pepper	¾ cup Pecorino Romano, pared into shavings with a potato peeler
a grating of fresh nutmeg	
½ cup Parmigiano-Reggiano, finely grated	**You will also need an ovenproof gratin dish 7 × 7 × 2 inches, lightly buttered.**
8 ozs. trimmed asparagus	
1½ tablespoons extra-virgin olive oil	Preheat the oven to 400°F.

First of all, place the milk, flour, and butter in a saucepan and mix over a gentle heat until the sauce begins to simmer and thicken. Season with salt and pepper and a good grating of nutmeg. After that, turn the heat down to its lowest setting and let the sauce cook for 3 minutes, then stir in the grated Parmigiano, remove from the heat, cover, and set aside while you prepare the other ingredients.

Prepare the asparagus by cutting the stalks diagonally into pieces roughly the same size as the rigatoni. Then take a 9-inch skillet, heat up the oil in it, and sauté the asparagus pieces for about 5 minutes, tossing them around the pan and keeping the heat fairly high so that they color at the edges. Add the tomatoes to the pan and let them bubble and reduce for about 1 minute. Then turn the heat off.

Next, cook the pasta in plenty of boiling salted water (to which a few drops of oil have been added) for 6 minutes only; then drain in a colander. Return the pasta to the saucepan, add the sauce and the asparagus mixture, and mix thoroughly. Taste to check the seasoning, pour the whole lot into the gratin dish, sprinkle with the shavings of Pecorino, and bake in the oven for 8 to 10 minutes. Serve straightaway.

———————— ◊ ————————

Savory Feta Cheesecake

.

SERVES 6 TO 8

The idea of a savory cheesecake is for me quite new. In the testing, I've had several misses, mainly because they somehow tasted too cheesy. This one, however, is a real winner. Feta cheese lightened with yogurt makes a lovely cool summer cheesecake, just right served with a salad for a light lunch, and a really wonderful accompaniment would be the Preserved Pickled Peaches on page 182.

FOR THE BASE:

1½ cups fresh breadcrumbs

½ cup Pecorino Romano, finely grated (if not available, you can use Parmigiano-Reggiano)

¼ stick butter, melted

freshly ground black pepper

FOR THE FILLING:

2 teaspoons fresh lemon juice

1 tablespoon water

2 teaspoons unflavored gelatin

8 ozs. feta cheese

1 cup whole-milk plain yogurt

1 cup soft farmer's cheese

½ cup chopped fresh chives

3 scallions, finely sliced

freshly ground black pepper

2 egg whites

You will also need an 8-inch springform cake pan. If it is less than 2 inches deep, line the sides with baking parchment to give a depth of 2 inches.

Preheat the oven to 400°F.

Begin by putting the breadcrumbs in a bowl and adding the cheese, the melted butter, and a seasoning of pepper (no salt because the cheese is quite salty). Now press the crumb mixture into the base of the prepared pan, pressing it firmly flat with the back of a spatula. Pop it into the oven on a high shelf and bake for about 15 minutes, or until it is crisp and toasted golden brown. Then remove from the oven.

Now for the filling: Measure the lemon juice and water into a small teacup, sprinkle in the gelatin, and set aside for 10 minutes to allow the gelatin to soak into the liquid. Then place the cup in a small saucepan containing a little water and allow it to simmer gently until the gelatin is completely liquid and has turned transparent. Leave the cup in the warm water so that it doesn't set.

Meanwhile, make the filling first by breaking up the feta cheese with a fork and then adding this to a food processor, along with the yogurt and farmer's cheese, and blending until completely smooth. Then transfer to a bowl and stir in the chives, the scallions, and some freshly ground pepper. Next, in a separate clean bowl, beat the egg whites with a wire whisk or an electric hand beater to the soft-peak stage.

Now you must act fairly quickly: Pour the gelatin through a strainer onto the cheese and stir to combine it thoroughly, then follow this with the beaten egg whites, first folding 1 tablespoon into the cheese mixture to loosen it, then stirring in the remaining whites. Pour the whole lot onto the cooled base, cover with plastic wrap, and transfer the cheesecake to the refrigerator to chill and set until needed.

Twice-Baked Goat's Cheese Soufflés *with* Chives

.

SERVES 4

Is there anyone who doesn't love to eat a fluffy cheese soufflé straight from the oven? But oh, the anxiety for the cook who has to commute to the kitchen to keep peering into the oven — and then finds that the guests all want to go to the bathroom the moment the soufflé gets to the table! Well, now you can relax, because twice-cooked soufflés can be made two or three days in advance (or even weeks if you want to freeze them). All you then do is turn them out onto a baking sheet and bake them 25 minutes before you need them. They are extremely well behaved when cooked, and although they may lose some of their puffiness if kept waiting, we have eaten them half an hour after cooking and they still taste great.

1 cup whole milk
1 small onion, cut in half
1 bay leaf
a grating of fresh nutmeg
a few whole black peppercorns
salt and freshly ground black pepper
¼ stick unsalted butter
¼ cup self-rising flour
2 large eggs, separated
1 tablespoon chopped fresh chives

4 ozs. peppered goat's cheese, cut into ¼-inch cubes

TO SERVE:
freshly grated Parmigiano-Reggiano

You will also need 4 ramekins, 3 inches across and 1½ inches deep, well buttered, a roasting pan, and a baking sheet.

Preheat the oven to 350°F.

Begin by placing the milk, the onion, the bay leaf, a good grating of nutmeg, a few whole peppercorns, and some salt in a small saucepan. Slowly bring to a simmer, then strain the mixture into a pitcher and discard the onion, bay leaf, and peppercorns. Rinse and dry the saucepan, place it back on the heat, and melt the butter in it. Stir in the flour and cook gently for 1 minute, stirring all the time, to make a smooth, glossy paste. Now add the hot milk, little by little, stirring well after each addition. When all the milk is incorporated, let the sauce barely bubble and thicken, then leave it on the lowest possible heat for 2 minutes.

Now take the sauce off the heat and transfer it to a large mixing bowl. Beat in first the egg yolks, then the chives. Mix everything thoroughly together and taste to check the seasoning. Finally, fold in three-quarters of the cubed goat's cheese.

Next, in another clean bowl, beat the egg whites with a whisk or a hand beater to the soft-peak stage. Then, taking one tablespoon at a time, fold the egg whites into the cheese-and-egg mixture, using cutting and folding movements so as not to lose the air. Now divide the mixture between the buttered ramekins, place them in a roasting pan, and pour about ½ inch of boiling water straight from a kettle into the pan.

Place the roasting pan on a high shelf in the oven and bake the soufflés for about 15 minutes, or until they are set and feel springy in the center (it is important not to undercook them at this stage, because on the second cooking they are going to be turned out). Don't worry if they rise up a lot — as they cool they will sink back. Remove them from the roasting pan straightaway, then cool and refrigerate until needed (they can also be frozen at this stage).

To serve the soufflés, preheat the oven to 400°F. Butter a baking sheet, then slide the point of a small knife around each soufflé, turn it out onto the palm of your hand, and place it the right way up on the baking sheet, keeping it well apart from its neighbors. Sprinkle the remaining goat's cheese on top of each one, then pop them into the oven on the middle shelf and bake for 20 to 25 minutes, or until they're puffy, well risen, and golden brown.

Using a spatula, slide each soufflé onto a hot platter and serve straightaway with some freshly grated Parmigiano sprinkled over. Serve on a salad of arugula dressed with Balsamic Vinaigrette Dressing (page 35), to which you have added 1 ounce chopped sun-dried tomatoes.

NOTE: If you don't like goat's cheese, use 4 ounces strong Cheddar instead. Also, if you wish, you can give the soufflés their second cooking in the dishes without turning them out. But I think it's more fun to turn them out, and that way you get nice crusty edges.

———————— ◊ ————————

Roasted Vegetable Couscous Salad
with Harissa-Style Dressing

·

SERVES 4 AS A MAIN COURSE OR 8 AS A FIRST COURSE

*T*his *salad is one of the best vegetarian dishes I've ever served. The combination of goat's cheese and roasted vegetables on a cool bed of couscous mixed with salad leaves and a spicy dressing is positively five-star.*

1 recipe roasted vegetables (see next recipe), with 1 small bulb fennel, chopped, substituted for the yellow pepper

FOR THE COUSCOUS:
2 cups couscous
2¼ cups boiling vegetable stock
salt and freshly ground black pepper
4 ozs. firm goat's cheese

FOR THE DRESSING:
½ cup extra-virgin olive oil
1½ teaspoons cayenne pepper
2 tablespoons ground cumin
3 tablespoons tomato paste
⅓ cup fresh lime juice (about 2 limes)

FOR THE SALAD:
3 ozs. mesclun

TO GARNISH:
1 tablespoon black sesame seeds

First, prepare the roasted vegetables (see next recipe), then remove them to a plate to cool. When you're ready to assemble the salad, place the couscous in a large flameproof bowl, pour the boiling stock over it, add some salt and pepper, stir it with a fork, and set it aside for 5 minutes, by which time it will have absorbed all the stock and softened.

Meanwhile, cut the cheese into sugar-cube-sized pieces. Make up the dressing by beating all the ingredients together in a bowl, then pour into a pitcher. To serve the salad, place the couscous in a large, wide salad bowl and gently fork in the cubes of cheese along with the roasted vegetables. Next arrange the salad leaves on top, and just before serving, drizzle a little of the dressing over the top, followed by a sprinkling of seeds. Hand the rest of the dressing around separately.

———————— ◇ ————————

Roasted Vegetable Couscous Salad with Harissa-Style Dressing

Roasted Mediterranean Vegetable Lasagne

.

SERVES 4 TO 6

*B*aked lasagne is the most practical of dishes — it can be prepared well in advance and needs no more than a shove in the direction of the oven at the appropriate time. But sadly, because of overexposure, the classic version is no longer the treat it used to be. This recipe follows the basic principles but incorporates the newer, smoky flavors of roasted Mediterranean vegetables. Even if you make it on a dull day, its dazzling colors will still be sunny.

FOR THE FILLING:

1 small eggplant

2 medium-sized zucchini

salt and freshly ground black pepper

1 lb. cherry tomatoes, skinned

1 small red bell pepper, deseeded and cut into 1-inch squares

1 small yellow bell pepper, deseeded and cut into 1-inch squares

1 large onion, sliced and cut into 1-inch squares

2 fat cloves garlic, crushed

2 tablespoons fresh basil, leaves torn so that they stay quite visible

¼ cup extra-virgin olive oil

⅔ cup pitted black olives, chopped

2 tablespoons capers, drained

¾ cup mozzarella, grated

FOR THE SAUCE:

¼ cup flour

3 tablespoons butter

2½ cups milk

1 bay leaf

a grating of fresh nutmeg

salt and freshly ground black pepper

½ cup grated Parmigiano-Reggiano

about 9 sheets oven-ready lasagne

FOR THE TOPPING:

2 tablespoons grated Parmigiano-Reggiano

You will also need a large, shallow baking pan and an ovenproof baking dish measuring 9 × 9 × 2 inches.

Preheat the oven to 475°F.

Prepare the eggplant and zucchini ahead of time by cutting them into 1-inch dice, leaving the skins on. Then toss the dice in about 2 teaspoons of salt and pack them into a colander with a plate on top and a heavy weight on top of the plate. Set them aside for an hour, so that some of the bitter juices drain out. After that, squeeze out any juices left and dry the dice thoroughly in a clean dish towel.

Now arrange the tomatoes, eggplant, zucchini, peppers, and onion in the baking pan. Sprinkle with the chopped garlic, basil, and olive oil, toss everything around in the oil to get a good coating, and season with salt and pepper. Now place the pan on the highest shelf of the oven for 30 to 40 minutes, or until the vegetables are toasted brown at the edges.

Meanwhile, make the sauce: Place all the sauce ingredients (except the cheese) in a small saucepan and stir continuously over medium heat until the sauce boils and thickens. Then turn the heat down to its lowest and let the sauce cook for 2 minutes. Now add the 3 tablespoons grated Parmigiano.

When the vegetables are done, remove them from the oven and stir in the chopped olives and the capers. Turn the oven down to 350°F.

Now, pour one-quarter of the sauce into the baking dish, followed by one-third of the vegetable mixture. Then sprinkle in a third of the mozzarella and follow this with a single layer of lasagne sheets. Repeat this process, ending up with a final layer of sauce and a good sprinkling of grated Parmigiano. Place the dish in the oven and bake for 25 to 30 minutes, or until the top is crusty and golden. All this needs is a plain lettuce salad with a lemony dressing as an accompaniment.

Pasta Puttanesca
(Tart's Spaghetti)

·

SERVES 2

*I*n Italian a puttana *is a "lady of the night," which is why at home we always refer to this recipe as tart's spaghetti. Presumably the sauce has adopted this name because it's hot, strong, and gutsy — anyway, eating it is a highly pleasurable experience. If you are a strict vegetarian, replace the anchovies with another 1½ tablespoons of capers.*

FOR THE SAUCE:	salt and freshly ground black pepper
2 tablespoons extra-virgin olive oil	
2 cloves garlic, finely chopped	a few drops of olive oil
1 fresh red chili, deseeded and chopped	salt
	8 to 10 ozs. spaghetti
1 tablespoon chopped fresh basil	(depending on how hungry you are)
1 can (2 ozs.) anchovies, drained	
1½ cups pitted black olives, chopped	
1½ tablespoons capers, drained	TO GARNISH:
1 lb. tomatoes, skinned and chopped	chopped fresh basil
1½ tablespoons tomato paste	lots of freshly grated Parmigiano-Reggiano

To make the sauce, heat the oil in a medium saucepan, then add the garlic, chili, and basil and cook these briefly till the garlic is pale gold. Then add all the other sauce ingredients, stir, and season with a little pepper — but no salt yet because of the anchovies.

Turn the heat to low and let the sauce simmer very gently without a lid for 40 minutes, by which time it will have reduced to a lovely thick mass, with very little liquid left.

While the sauce is cooking, take your largest saucepan, fill it with at least 3 quarts of hot water, and bring it up to a gentle simmer. Add a few drops of olive oil and a little salt and then, 8 minutes before the sauce is ready, plunge the spaghetti into the water. Stir well to prevent it from clogging together, then cook according to the package directions.

After that, drain it in a colander, return it to the saucepan *presto pronto,* and toss the sauce in it, adding the basil. Mix thoroughly and serve in well-heated bowls, with lots of grated Parmigiano to sprinkle over — and have plenty of gutsy, "tarty" Italian red wine to wash it down.

———————— ◊ ————————

Pasta Puttanesca

Frijolemole

.

SERVES 4 TO 6

This rather exotic title simply means "bean purée" — but a rather special one, made with garbanzo beans, chilies, fresh lime juice, and cilantro. It has a crunchy texture and is lovely for a first course or light lunch, served with some toasted bread and a salad.

1 cup dried garbanzo beans, soaked overnight in 2½ cups cold water	**1 large tomato, skinned and chopped**
1 tablespoon peanut oil	**½ teaspoon Tabasco**
1 medium Spanish onion, chopped	**1½ tablespoons chopped fresh cilantro**
2 cloves garlic, chopped	**2 tablespoons sour cream**
3 scallions	
1 fresh jalapeño or cayenne chili	**TO GARNISH:**
salt and freshly ground black pepper	**black olives**
2 tablespoons fresh lime juice	**flat-leaf parsley**

Begin by draining the soaked garbanzo beans and placing them in a saucepan with enough cold water to cover. Bring them to a simmer, cover, and simmer gently for about 45 minutes, or until they are tender when tested with a skewer.

Meanwhile, heat the oil in a small skillet and gently sauté the onion for 5 minutes, then add the garlic and cook for another 5 minutes. The scallions should now be trimmed and chopped small, and the chili should be split, deseeded under cold running water, and also chopped small. Don't forget to wash your hands straightaway!

When the garbanzo beans are ready, drain them in a sieve set over a bowl, then transfer them to a food processor, along with some salt, the sautéed onion and garlic, and any oil left in the pan. Now add the lime juice and blend until you have a smoothish purée — if it's too stiff add a couple of tablespoons of the cooking liquid from the garbanzo beans. What you need is a soft purée, like hummus in texture.

Now empty the contents of the processor into a bowl and add the tomato, chili, scallions, Tabasco, cilantro, and sour cream. Taste to check the seasoning and add a few more drops of Tabasco if it needs a little more kick. Cover the bowl and chill till needed. Serve garnished with black olives and some flat-leaf parsley.

———————————— ◊ ————————————

Cold Poached Egg Salad *with* Watercress Sauce

·

SERVES 3 AS A MAIN COURSE OR 6 AS A FIRST COURSE

This dish includes a kind of variation of a simple egg mayonnaise sauce, which I think makes the dish extremely attractive and even more delicious.

6 large fresh eggs	**1½ teaspoons mustard powder**
	freshly ground black pepper
FOR THE WATERCRESS SAUCE:	**1¼ cups peanut oil**
1 bunch watercress, dried on paper towels	**2 teaspoons wine vinegar**
2 large eggs	**1 teaspoon fresh lemon juice**
1 teaspoon salt	**TO SERVE:**
1 clove garlic	**assorted salad leaves**

Begin by poaching the 6 eggs: Fill a skillet with water to a depth of approximately 1½ inches and heat it to a temperature just sufficient to keep the water at a bare simmer. Break the eggs, 2 at a time, into the simmering water and let them cook for 3 minutes or so. As soon as they're cooked to your liking, use a slotted spoon to lift them from the water and transfer them to a bowl of cold water. Then cook the remaining eggs and leave them in the cold water while you prepare the sauce.

Separate off the watercress leaves and discard the stems. Break the 2 eggs into a food processor or blender. Add the salt, garlic, and mustard and a few twists of freshly ground black pepper, then switch on to blend these together. Next, pour the oil in a *thin* trickle through the feed tube or the hole in the top with the machine still switched on. When all the oil is in, add the vinegar, lemon juice, and watercress leaves, then blend again until the sauce takes on a lovely speckled green color. Place the sauce in a container and be sure to keep it refrigerated until immediately before serving.

To serve, place thinly sliced salad leaves around the edges of each plate to form a border, then arrange 1 or 2 eggs in the center of each plate and spoon the sauce over and around them. Serve with crusty whole-wheat bread.

— ◇ —

CHAPTER SEVEN

Summer Meat
and
Poultry

— ◇ —

Summer is the best time to cook and eat locally reared lamb if it is available, because this is lamb that has had the benefit of the luscious spring grazing and tastes all the better for it. Chicken, too, is good in summer, provided you look for that essential label "free-range" — under any other circumstances the season is irrelevant and so is the flavor. It is a constant refrain of mine, but I would rather not eat meat at all if it lacks quality or taste: better to eat it less often and pay more for quality.

One of the imponderables I had to face while writing a collection of recipes for summer was rainy days, and that is why this book contains a number of more exotic recipes, like the Sri Lankan Curry, which is made with coconut. If you haven't yet used fresh coconut for cooking, perhaps a rainy day is the time to get to grips with it. It's much more user-friendly than you may think (see the recipe on page 112): it really enhances curries *and* provides a delicious sambal to go with them.

Pork Saltimbocca

.

SERVES 2

This classic Italian recipe should be made with veal, but we find it tastes even nicer made with pork.

8 ozs. pork tenderloin, cut into 6 medallions 1 inch thick	**¾ cup Marsala wine**
salt and freshly ground black pepper	**1½ tablespoons olive oil**
6 slices prosciutto (about 2½ ozs.)	
6 large fresh sage leaves	**You will also need a 9-inch skillet and 3 wooden toothpicks.**

First of all, beat the pieces of meat out to make them a little thinner. I use a clenched fist to do this, but don't go mad and break the meat — it just needs to be flattened and stretched a bit. Season the meat with salt and pepper and then lay the slices of prosciutto on top of the pork (because they won't be precisely the same size, fold them and double over the pieces if necessary to make them fit). Now place a sage leaf in the center of each piece and secure it with half a toothpick, using it as you would a straight pin.

Next, measure the Marsala into a small saucepan and place it on a gentle heat to warm through. Now heat the oil in the skillet until fairly hot, then sauté the slices of pork (sage leaf side down first) for 2 minutes, then flip the pieces over and sauté for another 2 minutes. After that, pour in the hot Marsala and let it bubble and reduce for a minute or so until it becomes a syrupy sauce. Now transfer the pork to warm plates, remove the toothpicks, and spoon the sauce over. Serve with sautéed potatoes sprinkled with a few herbs before cooking, and a mixed salad.

◊

Baked Lamb *with* Rosemary *with* Red Currant *and* Mint Sauce

·

SERVES 6

*L*amb is in peak condition in midsummer, as it has then had the benefit of the sweet, young, spring grazing. At this time I would only serve it plain-roasted with a sauce of young mint leaves. But later on in the summer, or if you cannot obtain locally raised lamb, this is a fine way to cook and serve it: the foil-baking ensures that it stays juicy.

1 clove garlic	**FOR THE SAUCE:**
½ teaspoon coarse salt	**3 tablespoons good-quality red**
1 tablespoon extra-virgin	**currant jelly**
olive oil	**3 tablespoons red wine vinegar**
2 tablespoons chopped	**½ cup chopped fresh mint**
fresh rosemary leaves,	**salt and freshly ground black pepper**
plus 1 sprig of rosemary	
freshly ground black pepper	**You will also need a roasting pan.**
1 leg of lamb (4½ lbs.)	
1¼ cups dry white wine	Preheat the oven to 375°F.

First of all, crush the garlic and salt together to a purée, using a mortar and pestle, then add the oil, chopped rosemary, and a good seasoning of pepper and mix well. Next spread a large sheet of foil over the roasting pan, place the lamb on it, and stab the fleshy parts of the joint several times with a skewer. Now spread the rosemary mixture all over the upper surface of the lamb and tuck in a sprig of rosemary (as this makes a nice garnish later).

Then bring the edges of the foil up over the lamb, make a pleat in the top, and scrunch in the ends. This foil parcel should be fairly loose to allow the air to circulate. Bake the lamb for 2 hours, then open out the foil, baste the joint well with the juices, and return it to the oven for a further 30 minutes to brown. The above cooking time should produce a very slightly pink roast — you can cook it for more or less time, as you prefer.

Meanwhile, make the sauce by combining the red currant jelly and vinegar in a small saucepan and stirring over a gentle heat till the jelly melts into the vinegar (a wire whisk does this perfectly). Then add the chopped mint and some seasoning and pour into a pitcher — the sauce doesn't need to be warm.

When the lamb is cooked, remove it from the oven and allow it to rest for 20 minutes before carving. Discard the foil, spoon off the fat, and make some gravy with the juices left in the pan: Add the white wine, stir, and let it bubble until it has become syrupy. Season with salt and pepper if it needs it and pour into a warmed pitcher.

———————— ◊ ————————

Baked Lamb with Rosemary with Red Currant and Mint Sauce

Sri Lankan Curry

·

SERVES 4

T his is one of my favorite curries, made extra special by the use of fresh coconut, half of which goes into the curry and the rest of which is used to make the sambal on the opposite page. If you've never used a fresh coconut before, fear not — I have given very easy, straightforward instructions below.

3 tablespoons peanut oil	1 cinnamon stick
2 onions, chopped small	6 cardamom pods, crushed
1 large clove garlic, crushed	1½ teaspoons fenugreek powder
1½ lbs. boned shoulder of lamb (weighed after trimming), cut into cubes	salt and freshly ground black pepper
2 tablespoons flour	
1½ tablespoons Madras curry powder	TO GARNISH:
milk from 1 fresh coconut	2 hard-boiled eggs, halved
about 1 cup stock	1 medium onion, quartered and separated out into layers
1 cup finely grated fresh coconut	
1 can (15 fluid ozs.) coconut milk, unsweetened	

Preheat the oven to 300°F.

NOTE: Dealing with a fresh coconut (which does not, I admit, look user-friendly) is not as difficult as it seems. First push a skewer into the three holes in the top of the coconut and drain out the milk and reserve it. Then place the coconut in a plastic bag and set it on a hard surface — a stone floor or an outside pavement. Then give it a hefty whack with a hammer — it won't be that difficult to break. Now remove the pieces from the bag, and using a cloth to protect your hands, wedge the tip of a kitchen knife between the nut and the shell. You should find you can force the whole piece out in one go. Now discard the shell and take off the inner skin using a potato peeler. The coconut is now ready to use.

First heat 1 tablespoon of the oil in a large casserole, then add the onions and garlic and cook gently to soften for 5 minutes. Next, heat the remaining 2 tablespoons of oil in a skillet, and when it's nice and hot, quickly brown the cubes of meat (you will have to do this in two batches). Then sprinkle the flour and curry powder over the onions in the casserole and stir to soak up the juice. Cook gently for 2 minutes.

Now pour the fresh and canned coconut milk into a large measuring cup and add stock until the volume of liquid comes up to 3¼ cups. Slowly pour this into the casserole, stirring all the time. Next, stir in the grated fresh coconut and transfer the browned meat to the casserole. Finally, add the spices and season with salt and pepper. Bring to a simmer, cover, and cook in the center of the oven or at a low simmer on top of the stove for 2 hours. Five minutes before the end of the cooking time, remove the cinnamon stick and stir the hard-boiled eggs and onion pieces into the curry to warm through (the onions are not meant to be cooked). Serve with the Coconut Sambal (below) and Spiced Rice Pilaf (page 114).

———◇———

Coconut Sambal

SERVES 4

flesh of ½ fresh coconut, finely grated	**2 teaspoons fresh lemon or**
1 medium onion	**lime juice**
¼ teaspoon chili powder	**½ teaspoon salt**

Quite simply, grate the coconut and the onion straight into a bowl, then sprinkle in the chili powder, lemon juice, and salt. Stir to get everything nicely blended, then sprinkle just a tiny dusting of chili powder over the top, cover, and chill slightly until needed.

———◇———

Spiced Rice Pilaf

.

SERVES 4

The fragrance and flavor of an authentic spiced pilaf rice, made with the best-quality basmati rice, is so good it could be eaten just on its own! If cooking rice bothers you, follow these instructions and you'll never have a problem.

2 cardamom pods, crushed	1⅓ cups white basmati rice
¾ teaspoon cumin seeds, crushed	2½ cups boiling water
½ teaspoon coriander seeds, crushed	1-inch piece cinnamon stick
1 tablespoon peanut oil	1 bay leaf
1 small onion, finely chopped	salt

Use a mortar and pestle to crush the cardamom pods and the cumin and coriander seeds. Then warm a 10-inch skillet (with a lid) over medium heat, add the crushed spices (the pods as well as the seeds of the cardamom), turn the heat up to high, and toss the spices around in the heat to dry-roast them and draw out the flavor: this will take about a minute. After that, add the oil and the onion and fry the onion till lightly tinged brown.

Next stir in the rice — there's no need to wash it — and turn the grains over in the pan till they are nicely coated and glistening with oil. Then pour in the boiling water. Add the cinnamon, the bay leaf, and a good seasoning of salt. Stir once only, then put the lid on, turn the heat down to its very lowest, and let the rice cook for exactly 15 minutes. Don't remove the lid and *absolutely no stirring* at any stage from now on, because this breaks the grains and causes them to become sticky. After 15 minutes take the pan off the heat, remove the lid, and cover with a clean dish towel for 5 minutes before serving. Then empty the rice into a warmed platter or serving bowl and fluff up lightly with a fork before it goes to the table.

◊

Cilantro Chutney

SERVES 6

1 large bunch fresh cilantro, roughly chopped (about 2 cups)	**1 fresh chili, deseeded and chopped**
	1 clove garlic
1 tablespoon fresh lime juice	**¼ teaspoon sugar**
3 tablespoons water	**salt and freshly ground black pepper**

Place half the cilantro in a blender or a food processor, together with the lime juice, water, chili, and garlic, then blend till smooth. You'll have to do this with a few stops to scrape down the sides of the container. When the mixture is smooth, add the remaining cilantro and continue to blend until smooth again. Taste and flavor with sugar, salt, and pepper and keep in a small, covered bowl in the refrigerator until needed.

◊

Baked Thai Red Curry Chicken

.

SERVES 2

If you have some Thai Red Curry Paste (page 51) at hand, this makes a very speedy supper dish for two (or more) people. Serve the chicken with Spiced Rice Pilaf (page 114) and Cilantro Chutney (page 115).

1 split chicken breast on the rib	**TO GARNISH:**
salt	**a few sprigs of fresh**
2 teaspoons peanut oil	**cilantro**
2 tablespoons Thai Red	**1 lime, cut into quarters**
Curry Paste (page 51)	

About 1 or 2 hours before you need to cook the chicken, lay the breasts in a heatproof dish, then take a sharp knife and make four diagonal cuts across each breast. Sprinkle first with a little salt and then with the oil, rubbing the oil well into the chicken. Next spread the curry paste over the surface of each portion and rub that in well too. Cover with plastic wrap and refrigerate while the chicken soaks up all the flavors.

To cook the chicken, preheat the oven to 350°F. Place the dish on a high shelf and cook for 30 minutes, basting with the juices from time to time. Serve the chicken with the rice and Cilantro Chutney, as mentioned above, garnishing with sprigs of cilantro and some lime quarters to squeeze over.

◊

Liver *with* Melted Onions *and* Marsala

·

SERVES 2

Buying *liver cut as thinly as one would want is always difficult, so this recipe, which calls for liver cut into thin strips, avoids the problem. If you don't have Marsala, you can use any sweet wine that's handy.*

2 tablespoons olive oil	salt and freshly ground black pepper
3 medium-sized onions, halved and thinly sliced	8 ozs. lamb's or calf's liver
1 large clove garlic, crushed	1 tablespoon butter
1¼ cups Marsala wine	
2 tablespoons balsamic vinegar	**You will also need 2 medium skillets.**

In the first skillet, heat 1 tablespoon of the oil, then add the onions, and keeping the heat fairly high, toss them around to brown to a dark — almost black — color around the edges. Then add the garlic and toss that around the pan a bit. Now pour in the Marsala and balsamic vinegar. Bring everything to a simmer, then turn the heat down to its lowest setting and let it just barely bubble (without covering) for 45 minutes. Then season with salt and freshly ground pepper.

Meanwhile, prepare the liver by slicing it into approximately 1½-inch lengths, keeping the lengths very thin (about the size of thin french fries). When the 45 minutes are up, heat the remaining 1 tablespoon oil along with the butter in the other skillet, and when the butter foams, add the liver slices and sear them very briefly. They take only about 1 to 2 minutes to brown, so do be careful, as overcooking will dry them too much. As soon as they're ready, tip them into a warmed platter, pour the hot sauce and onions from the other skillet over them, and serve immediately. This is good served with Sliced Potatoes Baked with Tomatoes and Basil (page 65).

—————— ◊ ——————

Chicken *with* Sherry Vinegar *and* Tarragon Sauce

·

SERVES 4

*T*his is my adaptation of a classic French dish called poulet au vinaigre. *It's very simple to make: the chicken is flavored with tarragon leaves and simmered uncovered in a mixture of sherry vinegar and medium sherry, so that the liquid cooks down to a glossy, concentrated sauce. Note that this recipe will work only with authentic Spanish sherry. Serve some well-chilled Fino sherry as an aperitif — perfect for a warm summer's evening.*

2 tablespoons olive oil	**2 cups medium-dry Amontillado**
1 chicken (3½ lbs.), cut into 8 pieces, or	**sherry**
4 chicken breast halves	**2 tablespoons crème fraîche**
salt and freshly ground black pepper	
12 shallots, peeled and left whole	**TO GARNISH:**
4 cloves garlic, peeled and left whole	**8 small sprigs of fresh tarragon**
2 tablespoons fresh tarragon leaves	
½ cup sherry vinegar	**You will also need a 9-inch skillet.**

First of all, heat the oil in the skillet and season the chicken pieces with salt and pepper. Then, when the oil begins to shimmer, fry the chicken (in two batches) to brown well: remove the first batch to a plate while you tackle the second. Each piece needs to be a lovely golden-brown color. When the second batch is ready, remove it to the plate to join the rest. Then add the shallots to the pan, brown these a little, and finally add the garlic cloves and cook until they are pale golden.

Now turn the heat down, return the chicken pieces to the pan, scatter the tarragon leaves all over, then pour in the vinegar and sherry. Let it all simmer for a bit, then turn the heat to a very low setting so that the whole thing barely bubbles for 45 minutes. Halfway through, turn the chicken pieces over to allow the other sides to sit in the sauce.

When they're ready, remove them to a warm platter (right side up), along with the shallots and garlic. The sauce will by now have reduced and concentrated, so all you do is stir in the crème fraîche, taste and season as required, then pour the sauce all over the chicken and scatter with the sprigs of tarragon. This is lovely served with tiny new potatoes tossed in herbs, and some fresh peas.

——————— ◊ ———————

Chicken with Sherry Vinegar and Tarragon Sauce

Chicken Basque

.

SERVES 4

he delicious combination of chicken and rice, olives and peppers is typical of all the regions around the western Mediterranean, but to my mind this Spanish version, with the addition of spicy chorizo sausage and a hint of paprika, beats the lot. My interpretation of it also uses dried tomatoes preserved in oil to give it even more character. This recipe will provide a complete supper for four from the same pot — it needs nothing to accompany it!

1 chicken (3½ lbs.), cut into 8 pieces	¾ cup dry white wine
salt and freshly ground black pepper	1 tablespoon tomato paste
2 large red bell peppers	½ teaspoon hot paprika
1 very large or 2 medium onions	1 teaspoon chopped fresh herbs
2 ozs. sun-dried tomatoes in oil	½ cup pitted black olives, halved
2–3 tablespoons extra-virgin olive oil	½ large orange, cut into ½-inch wedges,
2 large cloves garlic, chopped	with peel left on
5 ozs. chorizo sausage, skinned and cut into ½-inch slices	
1 cup brown basmati rice	**You will also need a wide, shallow, 9-inch flameproof casserole with a domed lid, or failing that, any wide flameproof 5-quart casserole.**
1¼ cups chicken stock (made from the giblets)	

Start off by seasoning the chicken pieces well with salt and pepper. Next, slice the red peppers in half and remove the seeds and pith, then slice each half into six strips. Likewise, peel the onion and slice into strips of approximately the same size. The dried tomatoes should be drained, wiped dry with paper towels, and then cut into ½-inch pieces.

Now heat 2 tablespoons olive oil in the casserole, and when it is fairly hot, add the chicken pieces — two or three at a time — and brown them to a nutty golden color on both sides. As they brown, remove them to a plate lined with paper towels, using a slotted spoon. Next add a little more oil to the casserole, with the heat slightly higher than medium. As soon as the oil is hot, add the onion and peppers and allow them to brown a little at the edges, moving them around from time to time, for about 5 minutes.

After that add the garlic, chorizo, and dried tomatoes and toss these around for a minute or two until the garlic is pale golden and the chorizo has taken on some color. Next, stir in the rice, and when the grains have a good coating of oil, add the stock, wine, tomato paste, and paprika. As soon as everything has reached a simmer, turn the heat down to a gentle simmer. Add a little more seasoning, then place the chicken gently on top of everything (it's important to keep the rice down in the liquid). Finally, sprinkle the herbs over the chicken pieces and scatter the olives and wedges of orange in among them.

Cover with a tight-fitting lid and cook over the gentlest possible heat for about 50 minutes to 1 hour, or until the rice is cooked but still retains a little bite. Alternatively, cook in a preheated oven at 350°F for 1 hour.

CHAPTER EIGHT

ENGLISH JELLIES, CREAMS, *and* COMPOTES

———— ◇ ————

As a confirmed weight watcher *and* a lover of good food, I try my best to eat a dessert only when I am out for supper or at home at the weekend. But what so often disappoints me — particularly in restaurants — is that the dessert I have been anticipating with such eagerness is a real letdown. Menus nowadays contain not nearly enough fruit-based dishes, which are low on calories. Or if a dessert is going to be really rich, and squander millions of calories, it *must* be absolutely ace or it's such a waste!

For those of you with similar problems, I have in this chapter set about devising recipes that are lighter and in particular make the most of all the wonderful fruits and flavors of summer. English jellies (known as gelatin-based desserts in America) made with wine are great fun and look stunning (see the photograph on page 128), and oven-baked compotes seem to draw out the flavor of the fruits in a way that poaching never does. As for the creamier desserts — well, even here we've succeeded in lightening them, by the use of less fatty ingredients, such as yogurt, without sacrificing an iota of flavor.

————————————————

English Peach Wine Jellies *with* Peach Purée

·

SERVES 8

Now that there are several peach-flavored sparkling wines on the market, they can be made into lovely gelatin desserts that retain some of the bubble and sparkle of the wine. Topped with a peach purée, they make one of the nicest cool, light summer desserts you can imagine.

2 large or 3 small limes	a squeeze of lime juice
2½ cups water	a little superfine sugar to taste
½ cup superfine sugar	
3½ envelopes unflavored gelatin	
1 bottle (750 milliliters) good-quality sparkling peach wine	**TO GARNISH:**
	8 strawberries

FOR THE PEACH PURÉE:	
4 ripe peaches (or nectarines)	**You will also need**
	8 wineglasses (1-cup size).

Take a parer or potato peeler and pare off the outer zest of the limes, being careful to take as little of the white pith as possible. Now place the lime zest in a saucepan with 2½ cups water and the sugar and bring it to a boil very slowly so that the lime has a chance to infuse. Then remove the pan from the heat and stir in the gelatin. Leave it to stand, stirring occasionally, until the gelatin has dissolved — about 10 minutes.

Next, squeeze the juice from the limes and add it to the mixture. Pour the whole lot into a large bowl — straining out the lime zest, which is no longer needed — and leave the mixture until it becomes syrupy, which will take about 45 minutes to 1 hour. After that, uncork the wine and gently stir it into the gelatin mixture, a little at a time. Pour the mixture into the glasses, cover each one with plastic wrap, and chill for several hours, until set.

You need to make the peach purée just before serving. First make a cut all around each peach, then give a little twist to separate the halves. Remove the pits, then bring a saucepan of water to a boil and pop the peach halves in for about 1 minute. After that, remove them with a slotted spoon and slip the skins off. Now transfer the peaches to a food processor, add a little lime juice and sugar to taste (it's difficult to be specific here because peaches vary so much), and process to a purée. Before serving, spoon the peach purée over the surface of each glass as a topping and garnish each one with a fresh strawberry to decorate.

◇

Italian Rice Creams *with* Raspberry Purée

·

SERVES 6

For those who get nostalgic for the rice puddings of their childhood, this is the adult answer, a more sophisticated and modern interpretation. Later on in the summer different fruits can be used for the purée, such as blackberries or red currants.

3¾ cups milk	**FOR THE RASPBERRY**
⅓ cup superfine sugar	**PURÉE:**
¼ whole nutmeg, freshly	3 cups raspberries
grated	⅓ cup superfine sugar
4-inch strip lemon zest	
½ cup Italian arborio rice	
⅔ cup heavy cream	**TO GARNISH:**
1 envelope unflavored	**sprigs of mint**
gelatin	
1 large egg yolk	
1 tablespoon butter	**You will also need 6 ramekins,**
3 drops of pure vanilla	**3 inches across and 1½ inches deep,**
extract	**lightly buttered.**

First, pour the milk into a saucepan and add the sugar, nutmeg, and lemon zest. Stir and bring everything to a simmer, then add the rice, giving it several good stirs. Then turn the heat down to its very lowest setting, put a lid on, and leave it for about 40 to 50 minutes, giving it a stir every now and again. If the heat is not low enough, you may need to use a heat diffuser. What you need to end up with is a mixture where most of the liquid has been absorbed.

About 10 minutes before the end of the cooking time, measure the cream into a pitcher and beat the gelatin into it to soak. Then, when the rice is ready, pour the cream and gelatin mixture into it, followed by the egg yolk, butter, and vanilla extract, and stir to mix everything very thoroughly, still keeping the heat very low. When it is all heated through — after about 2 minutes — remove from the heat and pour the mixture into the ramekins. Leave them to cool completely, then cover with plastic wrap and chill till needed.

To make the raspberry purée, simply place the raspberries and sugar in a blender and process to a purée, or else press through a fine sieve. Cover till needed.

To turn out the rice creams, slide a small spatula around the edges and ease the creams away from the sides using your finger. Invert onto small plates by giving a hefty shake.

Serve with the raspberry purée poured over and garnish with sprigs of mint.

———————— ◊ ————————

A Terrine *of* Summer Fruits

.

SERVES 8

This one is a stunner — *see for yourself in the photograph. It's also dead easy to make and slices like a dream, a lovely, fresh-tasting summer dessert. Note: It's important to have two heavy cans on hand, because the terrine needs to be weighted while it is setting.*

FOR THE FRUIT:	**2 envelopes unflavored gelatin**
3 cups small strawberries	**1 tablespoon fresh lime juice**
2 cups raspberries	
1 cup each of blackberries, red currants, and blueberries (or any other combination you like)	
2 cups sparkling rosé wine	**You will also need 2 loaf pans 9 × 5¼ × 3 inches, preferably nonstick but**
¼ cup superfine sugar	**anyway with a good surface.**

First, prepare the fruit: Remove the stems and halve the larger strawberries. Then mix the fruits together in a large bowl, being very gentle so as to avoid bruising them.

Now in a small saucepan heat half the rosé wine till it begins to simmer, then stir in the sugar and gelatin. Make sure that everything has dissolved completely before adding the remaining wine and the lime juice. Then pour the liquid into a pitcher and allow it to cool. While that's happening, lay the mixed fruit in a loaf pan — and it's worth arranging the bottom layer with the smallest, prettiest-shaped fruit, as this will be on top when the terrine is turned out.

Next pour all but ⅔ cup of the liquid over the fruit. Now lay a sheet of plastic wrap over the pan, place the other pan directly on top, and put two unopened cans of tomatoes or something similar to act as weights into the top pan. Put the whole lot into the refrigerator for about 1 hour, or until it has set. Then warm up the remaining wine mixture and pour it over the surface of the terrine. Recover with plastic wrap and refrigerate overnight to set firm.

When you are ready to serve, turn out the terrine by dipping the pan very briefly in hot water and inverting it onto a plate. Use a very sharp knife (also dipped first into hot water) to cut it into slices. Serve with chilled heavy cream, crème fraîche, or plain yogurt.

—————————— ◊ ——————————

A Terrine of Summer Fruits

Summer Fruit Compote

·

SERVES 6

Any mixture of fruit can be used for this, but remember that the flavor of red currants does tend to dominate — so if you're using them, use just a half quantity compared with the other fruits.

3 peaches
6 apricots
6 large plums
2 cups blueberries
¼ cup sugar
1½ cups raspberries

You will also need a shallow baking dish. I use a 12-inch round dish.

Preheat the oven to 350°F.

First, prepare the fruit. Halve each peach by making a slit all around through the natural crease, then simply twist in half and remove the pit. Cut the halves into three pieces each and place them in the baking dish. After that, do the same with the apricots. If the apricots are large, slice the halves into two; if they're small, leave the halves whole. Repeat this with the plums, but if they're clinging too tightly to their pits, you may find it easier to slice them into quarters on the pit and pull each quarter off.

Add the apricots and plums to the peaches in the dish, followed by the blueberries. Now sprinkle the sugar over them, place the dish in the center of the oven, and let the fruits bake (without covering) for 25 to 30 minutes, or until they are tender when tested with a skewer and the juices have run. Then remove them from the oven and gently stir in the raspberries, tipping the bowl and basting them with the hot juices. Taste to check the sugar and add more if you think it needs it, then cool the compote and chill in the refrigerator. Serve with crème fraîche, cream, or vanilla ice cream.

NOTE: If you want to make the compote entirely with soft berries, it needs only 10 minutes in the oven.

———————— ◊ ————————

Summer Fruit Compote Scented *with* Lemongrass

·

SERVES 6

Thisis unusual and subtle — the scent of the lemongrass is barely there, but it does add a very interesting dimension.

2 finger-thin stems lemongrass, trimmed (page 10)	Any fruit compote combination (see previous recipe)
¼ cup superfine sugar	

Cut the lemongrass into 1-inch pieces and place them in a food processor or a blender together with the sugar. Turn the motor on and process until the lemongrass is so small that it disappears into the sugar. Add this mixture to the fruit and cook as described in the previous recipe, remembering to add soft fruit only after cooking.

———————— ◊ ————————

Vanilla Cream Terrine *with* Raspberry Coulis

·

SERVES 6

This is one of those oh-so-simple-but-oh-so-good desserts that offer precisely the right background to vivid, rich raspberries.

FOR THE TERRINE:	**3 tablespoons superfine sugar**
2 envelopes unflavored gelatin	
2 cups heavy cream	
⅓ cup superfine sugar	**TO GARNISH:**
2 cups plain whole-milk yogurt	**1½ cups raspberries**
2 teaspoons pure vanilla extract	**fresh mint leaves**
FOR THE RASPBERRY COULIS:	**You will also need a plastic freezer box**
2 cups raspberries	**measuring 4 × 4 × 4 inches.**

Begin by placing the gelatin in a cup together with 6 tablespoons of the cream and leaving it to soak for 10 minutes. Meanwhile, place the rest of the cream in a saucepan with the sugar and heat gently till the sugar has dissolved (it's important not to overheat the cream). Next add the soaked gelatin to the warm cream and stir everything over the heat for a few seconds. Now remove the cream mixture from the heat.

In a mixing bowl, stir the yogurt and vanilla together, then pour in the gelatin cream mixture through a strainer. Mix very thoroughly and pour the whole lot into the plastic box, allow to cool, then cover and chill in the refrigerator for at least 4 to 6 hours or preferably overnight, until it's set.

Meanwhile, make the coulis by placing the raspberries in a bowl and then sprinkling them with the superfine sugar. Leave to soak for 30 minutes, and then you can either strain them directly back into the bowl or, to make the straining easier, process them first, then strain into the bowl. Taste to check that you have added enough sugar, then pour into a pitcher and chill until you're ready to serve the terrine.

To serve, turn the terrine out onto a board, first sliding a spatula around the edges to loosen it, then giving it a hefty shake to turn it out. Cut into six slices and arrange each slice on a plate. Spoon a little coulis over the top left-hand corner and the bottom right-hand corner of each one and decorate with the fresh raspberries and mint leaves.

———————— ◊ ————————

Vanilla Cream Terrine with Raspberry Coulis

Rhubarb Compote

·

SERVES 3

Sometimes the simplest recipe can be a star if it's done properly. Rhubarb suffers from being overboiled and smashed to a pulp, but if you cook it gently in the oven with just sugar and no water, it will slowly release its juice, keep its chunky shape — and taste wonderful.

Mix 1½ pounds rhubarb with ⅓ cup superfine sugar and bake in a shallow baking dish, without covering, in a preheated oven at 350°F, for 30 to 40 minutes. For other variations you could add the grated zest and juice of 1 large orange, or 1 heaping teaspoon of grated fresh ginger (the ginger flavor works best, I think, with soft brown rather than white sugar).

VARIATION
Rhubarb Yogurt Fool

For this simple but so-lovely dessert, make a Rhubarb Compote as above, then purée it in a food processor together with ¾ cup plain yogurt. Garnish with some preserved ginger or a slice of orange.

————————— ◊ —————————

Compote *of* Fresh Figs *in* Muscat Wine *with* Vanilla Custard

·

SERVES 4

Agood way to serve figs that are unripe is to lightly poach them in a sweet, raisiny Muscat wine — Beaumes de Venise, or else a more modest Spanish, Italian, or California equivalent.*

½ **bottle Muscat wine**	**FOR THE CUSTARD:**
(375 milliliters)	**1 vanilla bean (after using for the figs)**
1 strip of lemon zest	**1¼ cups milk**
1 vanilla bean	**3 egg yolks**
8 plump fresh figs	**1½ teaspoons cornstarch**
	1 tablespoon mild honey

What you need to do is select a saucepan or skillet, with a lid, large enough to hold the figs in a single layer. Pour the wine into the pan, add the lemon zest and vanilla bean, and bring it to a simmer. Now wash the figs and stab each one two or three times with a skewer. Then, using a long-handled spoon, lower them into the simmering liquid, stem side up. Cover and cook very gently for 5 to 10 minutes, or until they are absolutely tender.

Now use a slotted spoon to remove them from the liquid to a shallow platter, where again they can sit in a single layer. Then scoop out the lemon zest and the vanilla bean (reserving this for use later) and boil the liquid rapidly until it has reduced to half its original volume. Pour it over the figs, leave to cool, and then chill until needed.

To make the custard, wipe the vanilla bean, split it down its length, and place it in a saucepan along with the milk. Heat it very gently and, while it's heating, beat the egg yolks, cornstarch, and honey together in a bowl. When the milk has come slowly to a boil, remove the vanilla bean and pour the hot milk onto the egg mixture, beating it in as you pour. Then return the whole mixture to the saucepan and put it back on the heat, stirring gently until it has thickened and almost reached the boiling point. Now pour the custard into a pitcher, cover with plastic wrap, leave to cool, and then chill. Remove from the refrigerator 1 hour before serving. Serve handed around to pour onto the figs.

NOTE: Vanilla beans can be wiped clean, stored in a jar, and used again and again.

◇

Fresh Peaches Baked *in* Marsala *with* Mascarpone Cream

·

SERVES 6

This combination of fresh, ripe peaches and the luscious flavor of Marsala wine makes a supremely good summer dessert that has the added advantage that it can be made well in advance. Mascarpone cream cheese has a rich dairy flavor, but it does tend to be a bit heavy, so mixing it with an equal quantity of plain yogurt lightens the texture without loss of flavor.

FOR THE PEACHES:

6 firm ripe peaches

3 tablespoons superfine sugar

1¼ cups sweet Marsala wine

1-inch piece cinnamon stick

1 vanilla bean

1½ teaspoons arrowroot

FOR THE MASCARPONE CREAM:

6 tablespoons mascarpone

6 tablespoons plain whole-milk yogurt or sour cream

a few drops of pure vanilla extract

1 tablespoon superfine sugar

You will also need a shallow baking dish.

Preheat the oven to 350°F.

Begin by halving the peaches and removing their pits, then place the halves in a bowl, pour boiling water over them, and after 30 seconds, drain them and slip off their skins. Now place the peach halves in the shallow baking dish, mix the sugar and Marsala in a pitcher, and pour over the peaches. Add the cinnamon stick and vanilla bean to the dish, then place it on the center shelf of the oven and bake without covering for 35 to 40 minutes. Then remove the peaches from the oven, discard the cinnamon stick, and drain off all the juices into a small saucepan. Mix the arrowroot with a little cold water and then add it to the saucepan and beat over a gentle heat until slightly thickened. This will happen as soon as it reaches the simmering point. Then pour it back over the peaches and leave to cool. When it has cooled, cover and refrigerate for 24 hours to allow the flavor to develop fully.

To make the mascarpone cream, simply beat all the ingredients together thoroughly and pile into a pretty serving bowl to hand around separately.

———————— ◊ ————————

Fresh Peaches Baked in Marsala

CHAPTER NINE

ICES
and
GRANITAS

───────── ◊ ─────────

This is a huge subject, and this chapter can do no more than offer you an introduction and encouragement to go more deeply into it.

No ice creams, however good they are, can beat a homemade ice cream. Even if you don't own an ice-cream maker, hiking the ice out of the freezer and giving it a quick stir isn't really a bother provided you set a timer to remind you to do it! The only other thing you must remember to do is to transfer the ice cream to the refrigerator to allow it to soften before serving. These times will vary but are given in each recipe. I shouldn't really be partial, because all the recipes in this chapter are favorites of mine, but if you want to give yourself a treat try the Caledonian Ice Cream (page 142). It's a winner.

NOTES ON MAKING ICE CREAM
Ice-Cream Makers

There are several ice-cream makers now available. The most efficient — and expensive — kind makes the ice cream from start to finish in approximately 30 to 40 minutes. This has its own built-in freezing device, therefore all you then do is transfer the finished ice cream to a plastic box for storing in the freezer or refrigerator till needed. If you're an ice-cream addict and make a lot of home-made ice cream, it would be worth the expense, though remember that machines always need somewhere to live, and space could be a problem.

The second kind of ice-cream maker is simply a machine that does the churning. The canister that holds the ice cream while it's churning has to be stored in the freezer and removed only when you need to actually churn it. The mixture then goes in and the machine churns it for 30 to 40 minutes, until the ice cream is thick. Then it is transferred to a plastic box and stored in the freezer if it's not going to be eaten straightaway. The canister is then washed, dried, and returned to the freezer until next needed for ice-cream making. It requires at least 12 hours in the freezer to become capable of freezing, and often — if a large quantity of ice cream is needed in one go — it's worth having two canisters so that you always have a standby. What is important is that the size of the canister must be larger than the amount of ice cream, because during churning the volume increases.

Making Ice Cream Without an Ice-Cream Maker (Freezer Method)

To make ice cream without an ice-cream maker you need a shallow plastic freezer box (with a lid) of 9-cup capacity — this works out at 8 × 8 inches × 2½ inches deep. The shallowness enables the freezing to happen more quickly and also makes the beating easier, as the beater can go down straight into the box.

It's a very easy process: All you do is pour the mixture into the box, put the lid on, and place it in the freezer for about 3 to 4 hours (it's impossible to be too precise because freezers vary). What you need is a mixture that is half frozen — the particles around the edges will be frozen solid, but the center will still be soft. At this stage you remove it from the freezer and, using a hand whisk, beat the frozen bits back into the soft bits till you get a uniform texture. Then the lid goes back on, the ice cream is frozen again, and the same process is repeated 3 hours later. After the second beating, the ice cream is ready and can be returned to the freezer until it's needed. Incidentally, it's a good idea to arm yourself with a kitchen timer to remind you to remove the ice cream and beat it at the various stages.

Serving Ice Cream

Serving ice cream is another of those minefields where guidelines are tricky because fridge temperatures vary. The average time for an ice cream to "come back" from being frozen is 40 minutes in the refrigerator. Don't be tempted to speed this up by bypassing the refrigerator and putting it straight into room temperature, as all this does is melt the outside edges and leave the center rock-hard.

Strawberry Granita

·

SERVES 8

This is the recipe to make when there's a real glut of ripe strawberries. It's a much nicer way to conserve them than simply freezing them. It looks like sparkling jewels when you serve it in tall glasses — and it contains hardly any calories!

4 cups ripe strawberries	**3 tablespoons fresh lemon juice**
⅔ cup superfine sugar	**You will also need a plastic freezer box**
2½ cups water	**8 × 8 × 2½ inches.**

First hull the strawberries, then put them in a colander and rinse them briefly with cold water. Drain well and dry them on paper towels before transferring them to a food processor or blender. Blend them to a smooth purée, then stop the motor, add the sugar, and blend again very briefly. After that add the water and lemon juice, blend once more, then pour everything into a fine sieve set over a bowl. Rub the purée through the sieve, then pour it into the freezer box, cover with a lid, and put into the freezer for 2 hours.

By that time the mixture should have started to freeze around the sides and base of the container, so take a large fork and mix the frozen mixture into the unfrozen, then recover the box and return it to the freezer for another hour. After that repeat with another vigorous mixing with a fork, cover again, and re-freeze for a further hour. At this stage the mixture should be a completely frozen snow of ice crystals and is ready to serve. It can remain at this servable stage in the freezer for a further 3 to 4 hours, but after that the ice will become too solid and it will need putting in the main body of the refrigerator for 30 to 40 minutes, or until it is soft enough to break up with a fork again.

I like to serve the granita in small, narrow, unstemmed glasses — but any wineglasses will also do, so the sparkling color can be seen in all its glory.

———————— ◊ ————————

Strawberry Granita

Caledonian Ice Cream

SERVES 8

This is, quite simply, a knockout ice cream — one of the best I've ever tasted. I am indebted to the Ubiquitous Chip restaurant in Glasgow, which very kindly let me have the recipe. The nutty, caramelized oatmeal gives a wonderful flavor and texture to the ice cream, and the whole thing makes a sublime partner to all summer fruits and compotes.

FOR THE CARAMELIZED OATMEAL:

⅓ cup superfine sugar

¼ cup water

½ cup steel-cut oats

FOR THE SYRUP:

½ cup superfine sugar

¼ cup water

FOR THE ICE CREAM:

2½ cups heavy cream

½ teaspoon pure vanilla extract

You will also need a loaf pan measuring 9 × 5¼ × 3 inches and a small baking sheet brushed with oil.

Start off by making the caramelized oats. Put the ⅓ cup of sugar and ¼ cup water in a small saucepan over a low heat and leave it for 5 minutes. Then take a medium-sized skillet, place it over medium heat, and when the pan is hot, add the oats and swirl them around the pan constantly so that they brown evenly, which they will do in about 5 minutes. Remove the oats to a plate to keep them from becoming overbrown. By now the sugar in the saucepan will have dissolved, so you can turn the heat right up and let it boil (watching it like a hawk) until it begins to turn a rich caramel color, rather like dark, runny honey.

As soon as it reaches that stage, stir in the toasted oats, remove from the heat, and quickly pour the mixture over the oiled baking sheet, then set it aside to get cold and firm (about 15 minutes). Now take off small pieces at a time and pound them in a mortar with a pestle until the mixture resembles something the size of coarse salt crystals. Place in a bowl and keep covered until you're ready to make the ice cream.

To make the sugar syrup, measure the ½ cup sugar and water into a small saucepan, place it over a gentle heat, and stir until the sugar has dissolved, about 5 minutes. Then remove it from the heat and allow it to get completely cold.

Now to make the ice cream. Pour the cold syrup into a mixing bowl along with the whipping cream, add the vanilla, and beat with an electric hand beater until the mixture just begins to thicken and hold its shape. Then pour this mixture into an ice-cream maker and freeze-churn until it is firm but still pliable — this will take about 30 to 40 minutes. Now transfer it to a bowl and fold in the oatmeal mixture evenly, then spoon it into the pan, cover with a double thickness of foil, and freeze till needed.

To serve, remove the pan from the freezer to the refrigerator about 20 minutes before you need it. Then dip the base and sides of the pan in hot water for 20 seconds or so, loosen all around the edges with a spatula, and turn out onto a plate. Using a sharp knife dipped into hot water, cut the ice cream into slices and serve on large plates with either soft fruit or any of the compotes or coulis on pages 130–35.

If you don't have an ice-cream maker, you can make this ice cream as described at the beginning of this chapter — except that in this particular case the caramelized oatmeal must be folded in just before the final freezing.

VARIATION
Macadamia Praline Ice Cream
This can be made as above but with 6 ounces crushed Macadamia Nut Brittle (page 155) in place of the oat mixture.

———————— ◊ ————————

Lemon Meringue Ice Cream

·

SERVES 8 TO 10; MAKES ABOUT 2½ PINTS

This is sharp, very lemony, and most refreshing, truly an ice cream for summer. I have found that the shop-bought meringues actually work better than homemade ones for this, as they retain their crunchiness — which does make the whole thing easier to do!

FOR THE LEMON SYRUP:	4 large egg yolks
3 teaspoons cornstarch	1½ teaspoons cornstarch
¾ cup fresh lemon juice (4 to 5 lemons)	¾ cup superfine sugar
	¾ cup plain whole-milk yogurt
½ cup superfine sugar	
grated zest of 2 lemons	20 mini-meringues, broken into coarse chunks
FOR THE ICE CREAM:	
2 cups heavy cream	**You will also need a 2-quart plastic freezer box 8 x 8 x 2½ inches.**

First of all, make the lemon syrup: In a bowl, mix the cornstarch with 2 tablespoons of the lemon juice. Then, in a small saucepan dissolve the sugar with the remaining lemon juice over low heat (5 to 6 minutes), add the zest, bring to a simmer, and cook for 5 minutes. Pour this over the cornstarch mixture, return it all to the pan, and still keeping the heat low, cook for 2 more minutes, stirring, until thickened. Then let cool and set aside till required.

Now make the custard base for the ice cream. Place the cream in a saucepan and heat gently. Meanwhile, beat the egg yolks, cornstarch, and sugar together. Then, when the cream reaches a simmer, pour it over the other ingredients, still beating, return the whole lot to the saucepan, and bring back to a bare simmer, continuing to beat. Pour the thickened custard into a bowl, cover with plastic wrap placed directly on the surface of the custard, and set aside until cool.

When the mixture is cool, combine it with the yogurt, then pour this into the freezer box, cover, and freeze for 2 hours, or until the mixture is starting to freeze. After that, use an electric hand beater to beat again, while the mixture is still in the box. Refreeze, then after a couple of hours repeat the beating, this time adding the lemon syrup. Finally, lightly and evenly fold in the meringue pieces, put the lid back on, and freeze till needed. It will take a further 6 to 8 hours to freeze completely.

NOTE: The quantity of this ice cream is too much for a standard ice-cream maker.

———— ◊ ————

Rhubarb Crumble Ice Cream

·

SERVES 6 TO 8; MAKES ABOUT 2½ PINTS

This ice cream has been voted their number-one favorite by many of my friends who have tasted all the ice-cream recipes in this book.

FOR THE CRUMBLE:
⅔ cup flour
½ stick butter
¼ cup soft light brown sugar
½ teaspoon ground ginger

FOR THE ICE CREAM:
1 lb. trimmed rhubarb
1 cup sugar

1 tablespoon fresh lemon juice
2 cups heavy cream

You will also need a shallow 11 × 7-inch baking pan and a 2-quart plastic freezer box 8 × 8 × 2½ inches.

Preheat the oven to 375°F.

First of all, make the crumble by combining all the ingredients together in a bowl and using your hands to rub the butter into the flour so that the mixture comes together to form small, pea-sized balls of dough (rather as if someone had made a halfhearted attempt to make breadcrumbs from very fresh bread!). Now sprinkle this evenly into the baking pan and set aside.

Now cut the rhubarb into ½-inch lengths and place them in a large, shallow baking dish along with the sugar and lemon juice. Place the dish on a lower shelf in the preheated oven, with the pan containing the crumble mixture on the shelf above. The crumble needs to be baked for 10 minutes, then remove it from the oven and leave to cool. The rhubarb may need a further 15 to 20 minutes' cooking before it is completely tender. When it's cooked, take it out and leave it to cool a little before pouring it into a food processor or blender. Process until you have a smooth purée, then pour it into a pitcher, cover, and transfer to the refrigerator to chill.

Before making the ice cream, use your hands to break up the cooled crumble and restore it to small, pea-sized pieces (if they're too big, the pieces are unwieldy to eat in the ice cream; if they're too small, they disappear). Next, stir the cream into the rhubarb purée, pour into an ice-cream maker, and churn until the mixture has the consistency of softly whipped cream. Quickly spoon it into the plastic freezer box and stir in the crumble pieces. Put the lid on, then freeze for a minimum of 2 hours, or until the ice cream is firm enough to serve.

To make without an ice-cream maker, freeze the mixture (without the crumble) in the box for 3 to 4 hours, then beat and return to the freezer. Refreeze for a further 2 hours, then beat again and stir in the crumble before the final freezing. (See page 138 for notes on ice cream.)

(*continued on page 146*)

If frozen solid, the ice cream will need to be transferred to the main body of the fridge for about 25 minutes before serving to allow it to become soft enough to scoop.

Ice-Cream Sodas

An ice-cream soda is a cross between a drink and a sundae. This can be a matter of simply placing two scoops of ice cream in a sundae glass (or a tumbler will do), pouring ¼ cup of cordial over the ice cream, and adding a bottle of soda water — which will give it a beautiful frothy head.

Instead of soda and cordial you could pour in Coca-Cola or traditional lemonade for the same effect: what it must have is some fizz. You'll need to give everyone a straw and a long spoon.

For a more special ice-cream soda, make up some lemon syrup as for Homemade Lemonade (see page 87) and assemble as above.

— ◊ —

Hot Fudge Sundae

·

SERVES 6

This is the most sublime summer chocolate dessert, especially for eating out of doors — say, at a barbecue.

FOR THE FUDGE SAUCE:	FOR THE TOPPING:
1 can (5 fluid ozs.) evaporated milk	⅓ cup heavy cream, whipped, or ⅓ cup crème fraîche
8 ozs. good-quality semisweet chocolate	1 cup nuts (pecans, brazils, almonds, peanuts, hazelnuts, on their own or in combination), coarsely chopped and lightly toasted
18 scoops Very Easy Vanilla Ice Cream (page 154)	

The sauce can be made at any stage and kept covered in the refrigerator, then reheated. All you do is pour the evaporated milk into a small earthenware bowl, then break up the chocolate into small squares and add them to the milk. Place the bowl on a saucepan of barely simmering water and leave it to melt, stirring from time to time. It will take about 10 minutes to become a lovely fudgy mass.

To serve the sundaes, put three scoops of very firm, cold ice cream per person into tall glasses, followed by 2 tablespoons of hot fudge sauce, followed by 1 tablespoon whipped cream or crème fraîche. Finally sprinkle some chopped nuts over the top and serve absolutely immediately.

— ◊ —

Overleaf: Ice-Cream Soda

Strawberry Cheesecake Ice Cream

·

SERVES 8 TO 10; MAKES 3 PINTS

This is what I'd call half dessert and half ice cream. My niece Hannah and nephew Tom are chief ice-cream tasters in our family, and this one gets very high ratings indeed from them. It differs from others in this chapter in that it needs two hours out of the freezer and in the refrigerator to become soft enough to scoop, so don't forget to allow time for that. It won't taste nearly as good if it hasn't been allowed to soften.

FOR THE STRAWBERRY PURÉE:

¼ cup superfine sugar

¼ cup hot water

2 cups fresh strawberries, hulled

FOR THE CRUMBLE MIXTURE:

2 ozs. sweet meal biscuits

¼ cup chopped toasted hazelnuts

2 tablespoons butter, melted

FOR THE ICE CREAM:

⅔ cup heavy cream

4 large egg yolks

1½ teaspoons cornstarch

⅓ cup superfine sugar

1 lb. farmer's cheese

⅔ cup plain whole-milk yogurt

1 teaspoon pure vanilla extract

1 tablespoon fresh lemon juice

You will also need a shallow baking sheet and a plastic freezer box 8 × 8 × 2½ inches.

First of all prepare the strawberry purée. Make a sugar syrup by placing ¼ cup sugar and ¼ cup water in a small saucepan. Put it on a gentle heat and allow the sugar to dissolve completely, stirring from time to time — this will take about 5 to 6 minutes. When there are no sugar granules left, let it come to a simmer and simmer very gently for 5 minutes. Now pile all the strawberries into a food processor, add the syrup, and blend to a smooth purée. Then strain the purée through a fine sieve into a bowl to extract the seeds.

Now, to make the crunchy bits for the ice cream, preheat the oven to 375°F. Crush the sweet meal biscuits with a rolling pin — not too finely — then place them in a bowl and combine them with the hazelnuts and the 2 tablespoons melted butter. Mix everything together, spread the mixture out on the shallow baking sheet, and bake on the top shelf of the oven for exactly 5 minutes: put the timer on and watch carefully, because any more than 5 minutes will be too long. Then remove it from the oven and allow to cool.

Next, you need to make the custard base for the ice cream: Place the cream in a saucepan and heat gently. Meanwhile beat the egg yolks, cornstarch, and sugar together. Then, when the cream reaches a simmer, pour it over the egg yolk mixture (still beating). Return the whole lot to the saucepan and bring back to a bare simmer, keeping up the beating until the custard thickens slightly. Pour it into a bowl, cover with plastic wrap placed right on the surface of the custard, and set aside till cool.

After that, place the farmer's cheese, yogurt, vanilla, and lemon juice in a mixing bowl, add the cooled custard, and beat the whole lot together till smooth.

You can make the ice cream with or without an ice-cream maker. If you have one, freeze-churn the mixture in the ice-cream maker until thickened. Transfer the mixture to a plastic freezer box and quickly fold in the crumble mixture, followed by the strawberry purée, which should form ribbons of red through the ice cream. Freeze for 5 to 6 hours. If you do not have an ice-cream maker, pile the custard-and-cheese mixture into the plastic freezer box and freeze for approximately 3 hours (see page 139). Then beat again till soft. Re-freeze and repeat the process after 2 or 3 hours, then fold in the crumble mixture, followed by the strawberry purée as described above. Return the ice cream to the freezer box and freeze till needed. Transfer to the main body of the refrigerator 2 hours before serving.

◇

Coconut Ice Cream

.

SERVES 4 TO 6; MAKES 2 PINTS

*C*ream *of coconut makes an excellent ice cream. Serve it with Lime Syrup (page 153) — the combination is superlative.*

3 large egg yolks	**2 tablespoons fresh lime juice**
1½ teaspoons cornstarch	**1 can (15 fluid ozs.) cream of**
⅔ cup whole milk	**coconut, sweetened**
⅔ cup heavy cream	
½ teaspoon pure vanilla extract	**You will also need a plastic freezer box 6 × 8 × 2 inches.**

First whisk the egg yolks and cornstarch together in a mixing bowl. Place the whole milk and the heavy cream in a small saucepan and bring to a gentle simmer. Then pour the milk mixture over the yolks — whisking as you pour. Now return the egg and milk mixture to the saucepan and cook for 1 minute, stirring until the mixture thickens. It is important to keep stirring to make sure the mixture does not "catch" on the bottom of the pan. Then return it to the bowl and allow it to cool. When it is completely cold, stir in the vanilla extract and lime juice, followed by the contents of the can of cream of coconut (well shaken). Give it all a quick whisk so that it's thoroughly smooth.

Transfer it all to a plastic freezer box and put in the coldest part of the freezer for 3 hours, or until it becomes firm at the edges. At this stage, empty it out into a mixing bowl and beat with an electric hand beater to break down the ice crystals. Return to the freezer, repeat the process after another 3 hours, and then refreeze until needed. This can, of course, be made in an ice-cream maker, following the manufacturer's instructions. This ice cream can be served straight from the freezer.

◊

Coconut Ice Cream with Lime Syrup (pages 152, 153)

Lime Syrup

.

MAKES 1¼ CUPS

This is extremely simple to make. It also keeps well, so it can be made in advance. Serve it with Coconut Ice Cream (page 151).

½ **cup sugar**	**1 teaspoon arrowroot**
½ **cup water**	½ **cup fresh lime juice**
zest of 1 lime (removed with a potato peeler), cut into very fine strips	**(about 3 limes)**

Begin by putting the sugar and water into a small, heavy-based saucepan. Bring it very slowly up to a simmer, then stir to dissolve the sugar. Add the zest of lime and simmer very gently for 15 minutes without reducing the volume. Meanwhile, mix the arrowroot with the lime juice in a cup, and when the syrup is ready, pour it in, stirring all the time. Continue to heat it over a gentle heat and allow it to come back to a simmer — by then it will have thickened very slightly and become clear. Leave the syrup to cool and then refrigerate it in a sealed container; it keeps well for several days.

———————— ◊ ————————

Very Easy Vanilla Ice Cream

.

SERVES 8 TO 10; MAKES ABOUT 3 PINTS

**2 cans (14 ozs. each) sweetened
condensed milk**

1¼ cups half-and-half

2 cartons (8 ozs. each) crème fraîche

2 teaspoons pure vanilla extract

**You will also need a plastic freezer box
8 × 8 × 2½ inches.**

Simply put everything into a bowl and use an electric hand beater to mix all the ingredients thoroughly. Then pour the mixture into a plastic freezer box and place it in the coldest part of the freezer. After about 2 hours, or when the edges are starting to freeze, remove it and use the hand beater to give it another good mix and break down any ice crystals. Return to the freezer, then repeat the process after 3 more hours. Finally, return it to the freezer for a further 6 to 8 hours, by which time it should be at serving consistency. If you've made it a long time ahead and it's very hard, transfer it to the main body of the refrigerator for 30 minutes to soften enough to scoop.

NOTE: Because of the very high sugar content in condensed milk, this recipe is not suitable for ice-cream makers.

— ◊ —

Macadamia Nut Brittle

Although you can buy nut brittle nowadays, it's extra specially good if you make it yourself. It keeps well wrapped in foil in the refrigerator, so you can take out a little at a time to crush and sprinkle over ice cream. Any nuts can be used, but my personal favorite at the moment are macadamia nuts, which somehow seem more summery!

4 ozs. macadamia nuts
2⅓ cups sugar
1 cup water

You will also need a baking sheet and a 9-inch plate, lightly oiled.

Preheat the oven to 350°F.

Begin by spreading the nuts out over the baking sheet. Place them in the oven for 8 to 10 minutes, or until they are just pale golden (do put a timer on, and watch carefully, as too much browning will spoil the flavor).

Next, have at the ready a bowl filled with cold water, and a dish towel. Then proceed as follows: Put the sugar in a heavy-based saucepan over a very gentle heat and measure in the water. Then stir constantly to dissolve the sugar in the water. If a lot of sugar crystals stick to the side of the pan, use a wet pastry brush to brush them back down. You need to be very patient here and keep the heat low until all the sugar has completely dissolved — and this can take 10 to 15 minutes.

After that, you can stop stirring, bring the sugar to a boil, and boil until it is a light caramel color (the color of runny honey). If you are using a sugar thermometer, this will be when it reaches 340°F. It will take 10 to 12 minutes, but don't go away, as it needs constant watching.

When it is ready, cover your hand with the dish towel in case of splashes and put the base of the pan into the water in the bowl to stop the cooking. Now add the nuts, and as soon as the mixture has stopped bubbling, pour it onto the lightly oiled plate. If it goes brittle before it is out of the pan, put it back on the most gentle heat, then quickly pour it onto the plate. When it has cooled a little, you can press the nuts fully into the caramel, and when it is quite cold, remove it from the plate, wrap in foil, and refrigerate.

NOTE: If your saucepan looks as though it is caramelized for good, fear not: fill it with warm water and place over a gentle heat till the caramel melts away from the base and sides.

◊

CHAPTER TEN

SUMMER BAKING
and
DESSERTS

◊

The recipes in this chapter are basically aimed at complementing the glorious fruits of summer. And what better to make that than some good, old-fashioned farmhouse fruit pies now and then? Lately I've discovered how easy it is to make a one-crust pie. All you do is pile your fruit onto a large, thin sheet of piecrust pastry and simply fold the pastry round the fruit, leaving some of it exposed in the center (see the photograph on page 168). A good idea for a dull or rainy day is to use it to prepare enough piecrust for several pies and store them in the freezer so that you can make a fruit pie at a moment's notice all through the summer.

Then, when the soft fruits — the strawberries and raspberries, the red currants and blueberries — come into season, I can think of nothing nicer to serve with them than meringues. This time I've rung the changes and devised Caramel Meringues (page 162), which are sandwiched together not with cream but with a delectable mixture of Italian mascarpone and soft farmer's cheese, a substitution that preserves the *flavor* of the mascarpone but cuts down the high fat content.

Summer tea out in the garden is a civilized pastime, and another idea for making that a bit special is the superb Coconut Lime Cake (page 172), which underlines what a perfect combination of flavors coconut makes with lime.

Preceding pages: Summer Fruit Millefeuille (recipe on page 159)

Summer Fruit Millefeuille

.

SERVES 6

You can use store-bought puff pastry for this — it won't have as good a flavor as the quick flaky pastry below, which is made with butter, but the caramelizing will help the flavor, and it does cut down on the time.

FOR THE CARAMELIZED FLAKY PASTRY:	3 tablespoons flour
¾ cup flour, with a pinch of salt added	1 teaspoon pure vanilla extract
5 tablespoons butter, wrapped in foil and left in the freezer for 1 hour	TO FINISH:
1 tablespoon fresh lemon juice	¾ cup heavy cream
1 egg, beaten	1½ tablespoons superfine sugar
2 tablespoons confectioners' sugar	confectioners' sugar for dusting
FOR THE PASTRY CREAM FILLING	FOR THE FRUIT:
1 large egg plus 1 egg yolk	1¼ cups raspberries
2 tablespoons superfine sugar	1¼ cups strawberries, hulled
1 cup milk	½ cup red currants, stems removed

To make the pastry, first sift the flour and salt into a bowl. Then take the butter from the freezer and, holding it with foil, dip it into the flour and grate it on the coarsest blade of a grater — dipping it into the flour once or twice more until it is all in the bowl. Now take a spatula and flick the flour over the grated butter, cutting and tossing until the flour and butter look evenly blended. Next, sprinkle in the lemon juice. Then, using your hands, gently bring the dough together, adding a few drops of water to make a firm dough that leaves the bowl clean. Wrap it in plastic wrap and chill it in the refrigerator for 30 minutes. Meanwhile, preheat the oven to 425°F.

Next, take a rolling pin and a tape measure and roll the pastry out to a square measuring 12 × 12 inches. Using the rolling pin to roll the pastry around, carefully transfer it to the baking sheet. Prick the surface of the pastry with a fork and brush it all over with beaten egg, then place the baking sheet on a high shelf in the oven and bake for 10 to 12 minutes — but do watch it carefully (no answering the phone, etc.), because ovens do vary. What you need is a very brown, crisp finish.

Then, to get it extra-crisp, preheat the broiler to its highest setting, sprinkle the pastry with 1 tablespoon of the confectioners' sugar, and then literally flash it under the hot broiler — don't take your eyes off it till the sugar caramelizes, which it will do in just a few seconds.

Remove the pastry square from the broiler and, using a sharp knife, cut it into three equal strips. Turn them over, sprinkle the rest of the confectioners' sugar over the strips, and flash them under the broiler once again. Once the pastry has cooled on a wire rack, it is ready to use and can be stored in a plastic freezer box, with the layers separated with a strip of waxed paper. The pastry is very delicate, so handle it carefully, but if any strips do happen to break, don't panic — you can use them as bottom or middle layers of the millefeuille.

To make the pastry cream, break the egg into a medium-sized bowl, then add the egg yolk and sugar. Next, put the milk on to warm over a gentle heat while you beat the eggs and sugar together until the mixture becomes thickened and creamy — about 1 minute with an electric hand beater on low speed. Then sift in the flour and beat that in.

Now turn the heat up to bring the milk to boiling point, and then beat the milk into the mixture. After that, return the whole lot to the pan and continue to beat, this time with a wire whisk, over medium heat until the mixture becomes very thick. Keep beating all the time, because the mixture can catch very easily if you don't. As soon as a bubble on the surface bursts, remove the sauce from the heat and quickly pour it into a bowl, then stir in the vanilla extract. Cover the pastry cream with plastic wrap to keep a skin from forming and leave it to get completely cooled.

When you come to assemble the millefeuille (which shouldn't be before about an hour before you want to serve it), beat the heavy cream and superfine sugar together till fairly stiff, then fold the pastry cream into it. To assemble, place the bottom layer of pastry on a suitably sized plate or board and spread it with a quarter of the cream. Top this with half the fruit and a further quarter of the cream. Now place the next layer of pastry on top, pressing it gently down to fix it in place, and cover this with another layer of cream, followed by the rest of the fruit and the rest of the cream. Finally, arrange the last layer of pastry on top, dust with confectioners' sugar, and cut into thin slices, using your sharpest knife.

———————— ◊ ————————

Cheesecake
with Strawberry Sauce

.

SERVES 8

Whenever I see cheesecake on a menu, I'm filled with longing — there's something awfully comforting about cheesecake — but the question always arises as to whether it will or will not be cloying (and if it is, what a waste of calories!). This version is definitely not cloying: it's light in texture and, made with yogurt, a bit lighter on the calories, too.

FOR THE BASE:
6 ozs. sweet meal biscuits
½ stick butter, melted
½ cup coarsely chopped toasted hazelnuts

FOR THE FILLING:
12 ozs. farmer's cheese
1½ cups plain whole-milk yogurt
3 large eggs

¾ cup superfine sugar
1 teaspoon pure vanilla extract

FOR THE TOPPING:
6 cups strawberries, hulled
2 tablespoons superfine sugar

You will also need a 9-inch springform baking pan.

Preheat the oven to 300°F.

Begin by crushing the sweet meal biscuits in a food processor or with a rolling pin, then mix them with the melted butter and stir in the hazelnuts. Now press the mixture into the base of the springform pan and pop it into the preheated oven for 10 minutes while the filling is made.

To make the filling, first combine, in a food processor, the yogurt, farmer's cheese, eggs, sugar, and vanilla, and process everything together until silky smooth. Now pour this mixture over the crust base and place on the center shelf of the oven to cook for 1 hour, 15 minutes. At the end of the cooking time, turn off the oven but leave the cheesecake in the cooling oven to set until it's completely cooled (I find that this is the best method, as it prevents cracking). Remove the cheesecake from the oven and from the pan, transfer it to a plate, cover, and chill till needed.

For the topping, place one-third of the strawberries in a bowl, sprinkle them with the sugar, and leave to soak for 30 minutes. After that, pile the strawberries and the sugar into a food processor and purée, then pass the purée through a fine sieve to remove the seeds. To serve the cheesecake, arrange the remaining strawberries all over the surface, then spoon some of the purée over them and serve the rest of the purée separately.

◊

Caramel Meringues

.

MAKES 12 SINGLE MERINGUES

I'm quite sure that nothing, but nothing, provides a better accompaniment to the tart flavors of soft summer fruits than meringues, light as a whisper on the outside and with a marshmallow chewiness inside. This year I've been making caramel meringues, which are even nicer and never fail to produce gasps of delight when they appear.

FOR THE CARAMEL:

¼ cup sugar

FOR THE MERINGUES:

3 large fresh egg whites

½ cup superfine sugar

TO SERVE:

1 cup whipped cream, crème fraîche, or Mascarpone Cream (page 136)

You will also need a nonstick baking sheet measuring 15 × 15 inches.

Preheat the oven to 300°F.

First make the caramel: Put the sugar in a small, heavy saucepan and place it on a gentle heat — and stay watching it like a hawk: the sugar will eventually melt and dissolve. You can shake the pan, but don't stir. When the sugar becomes liquid, let it cook until it turns the color of dark, runny honey, then take the pan off the heat immediately. Now pour the caramel onto a plate, and as soon as it becomes cool enough to handle — set but not hard — loosen it from the plate, so that when it's completely hard it doesn't stick. After that break it into pieces and grind it to a fine powder with a mortar and pestle.

To make the meringues, place the egg whites in a clean bowl and, using an electric hand beater, beat until they form soft peaks that just slightly tip over when you lift the beaters. Next, beat in the superfine sugar, a tablespoon at a time, followed by the caramelized sugar, also a tablespoon at a time.

When everything is thoroughly blended, take tablespoons of the mixture and arrange these on the baking sheet, then place a second tablespoon of meringue on top of each one, to make twelve meringues in all. Then place them in the oven, straight away reduce the heat to 275°F, and leave them for 1 hour 15 minutes. After that turn off the oven and allow the meringues to cool inside until the oven is completely cold.

To serve, sandwich the meringues together with the whipped cream, crème fraîche, or Mascarpone Cream and serve them piled high — preferably on a cake stand — with a fruit compote in a separate bowl.

———————— ◊ ————————

American Muffins

.

MAKES 20 MINI-MUFFINS OR 6 MAN-SIZED MUFFINS

I love American home cooking, and one of the things I feel Americans are particularly good at is baking (both at home and commercially). The American muffin reigns supreme, not like the British bread version but more like superior fairy cakes — oh so much easier to make and so much more of a treat! Like many other things in America, they used to come big, but now that calorie counting is here to stay there are mini-versions, which means you can make lots of different bite-sized flavors. Although I think minis are more fun, it has to be admitted that my husband's cricket team prefer something more substantial, so I've given you a choice. The single basic mix will provide twenty mini-muffins or six man-sized muffins.

FOR THE BASIC MUFFIN MIXTURE:

1 cup flour

½ tablespoon baking powder

¼ teaspoon salt

1 large egg

3 tablespoons superfine sugar

½ cup milk

½ stick butter, melted and cooled slightly

½ teaspoon pure vanilla extract

You will also need 2 mini-muffin trays, each cup measuring about 1¾ × ¼ inches, or standard muffin trays. The muffins can be baked with or without paper muffin cups, which simply help to keep them fresh.

Preheat the oven to 400°F.

Start off by sifting the flour, baking powder, and salt into a large bowl. Then in a separate bowl mix together the egg, sugar, milk, melted butter, and vanilla extract. Now return the dry ingredients to the sieve and sift them straight onto the egg mixture (this double sifting is essential, because there won't be much mixing going on). What you need to do now is take a large spoon and fold the dry ingredients into the wet ones — quickly, in about 15 seconds. Don't be tempted to beat or stir, and don't be alarmed by the rather unattractive, uneven appearance of the mixture: this, in fact, is what will ensure that the muffins stay light.

Now fold whichever combination of fruits/nuts etc. you have chosen (see pages 165–66) into the mixture, again with a minimum of stirring: just a quick folding-in. Spoon in just enough mixture to fill each muffin cup (if you're not using papers, grease the trays well) and bake on a high shelf of the oven for 20 minutes for minis or 30 minutes for the larger ones or until well risen and brown.

Remove the muffins from the oven and let cool in their trays for 5 minutes before transferring to a wire rack (if they are in paper muffin cups remove them from the trays straightaway). Leave to get quite cold before icing.

◇

Blueberry *and* Pecan Muffins

.

MAKES 20 MINI-MUFFINS OR 6 MAN-SIZED MUFFINS

1 cup small blueberries	**FOR THE TOPPING:**
½ cup or 2 ozs. pecans, finely chopped	**2 ozs. or ½ cup pecans, finely chopped**
1 recipe Basic Muffin Mixture (page 163)	**10 brown sugar cubes, crushed**

Fold the blueberries and pecans into the muffin mix as described on page 163, spoon into the muffin cups, and top with chopped pecans and crushed sugar before putting into the oven.

◊

Fresh Apricot *and* Pecan Muffins *with* Cinnamon Icing

.

MAKES 20 MINI-MUFFINS OR 6 MAN-SIZED MUFFINS

3 fresh apricots, finely chopped	**FOR THE CINNAMON ICING:**
¼ cup or 1 oz. pecans, finely chopped and lightly toasted	**1 cup confectioners' sugar, sifted**
½ teaspoon ground cinnamon	**approximately 3 teaspoons water**
½ teaspoon pure vanilla extract	
1 recipe Basic Muffin Mixture (page 163), using half whole-wheat and half all-purpose flour	**2 teaspoons ground cinnamon**
	10 toasted pecans, cut in half

Fold the apricots, pecans, cinnamon, and vanilla into the muffin mixture, as indicated in the recipe on page 163. For the icing, mix the confectioners' sugar with the water and cinnamon and spoon a little onto each muffin when they are cold, then top with half a pecan.

◊

Blueberry and Pecan Muffins

Coffee *and* Walnut Muffins

.

MAKES 20 MINI-MUFFINS OR 6 MAN-SIZED MUFFINS

3 ozs. or ¾ cup walnuts, finely chopped	**FOR THE TOPPING:**
2 tablespoons instant coffee mixed with 1 tablespoon boiling water	**2 teaspoons instant coffee mixed with 1 tablespoon boiling water**
1 recipe Basic Muffin Mixture (page 163)	**1⅓ cups confectioners' sugar, sifted**
	10 walnut halves, chopped in half again

Fold the chopped walnuts and coffee mixture into the muffin mix as described on page 163, spoon into the paper muffin cups, and place in the oven. For the topping, blend the coffee mixture with the confectioners' sugar, then spoon a little onto each muffin when they are quite cool. Top with a piece of walnut.

◊

Blueberry *and* Cinnamon Muffin Cake *with* Streusel Topping

SERVES 8 TO 10

Having recently got totally hooked on making muffins, I realized that the muffin mixture could be baked in an ordinary cake pan and served cut into thick slices, either as a dessert — fresh, still warm from the oven, and topped with yogurt or crème fraîche— or as a cake for tea in the garden on a sunny day.

2 cups flour	**1 teaspoon ground cinnamon**
1 tablespoon baking powder	**¼ stick butter, at room**
½ teaspoon salt	**temperature**
½ teaspoon ground cinnamon	**⅓ cup brown granulated sugar**
2 large eggs	**½ cup chopped toasted**
⅓ cup superfine sugar	**hazelnuts**
¾ cup milk	**1 tablespoon cold water**
1 stick butter, melted	
2½ cups blueberries	**You will also need a 9-inch nonstick springform baking pan.**
FOR THE TOPPING:	
⅔ cup self-rising flour	Preheat the oven to 375°F.

In this recipe, you need to sift the dry ingredients twice, so place the 2½ cups flour, the baking powder, the salt, and the cinnamon in a sieve and sift them into a bowl. In another mixing bowl, beat the eggs, sugar, and milk together, then melt the butter and pour this into the egg mixture, beating once again.

Now sift the flour mixture in on top of the egg mixture and fold it in, using as few folds as possible (ignore the lumpy appearance at this stage, and don't be tempted to overmix). Fold in the blueberries and spoon the batter into the pan.

To make the topping, you can use the same bowl that the flour was in. Add the flour, the cinnamon, and the butter and rub the butter in until crumbly, then add the sugar and hazelnuts and mix well. Finally, sprinkle in 1 tablespoon of cold water, then press the mixture loosely together. Now sprinkle this mixture all over the cake. Bake on the center shelf of the oven for 1 hour 15 minutes, or until it feels springy in the center. Allow it to cool in the pan for 30 minutes before removing the sides of the pan. Then slide a spatula gently under the base and transfer the cake to a wire rack to finish cooling.

NOTE: I have several times placed the base of a springform pan the wrong way up by mistake, so be careful that you have it the right way up!

A Very Easy
One-Crust Pie

·

SERVES 6

This way of making an open-faced pie is blissfully easy — no baking pans and no top crust to be cut, fitted, and fluted. It looks very attractive because you can see the fruit inside, and because there is less pastry, it's a little easier on the waistline.

FOR THE PIECRUST PASTRY:

1⅓ cups flour

¾ stick butter or margarine, at room temperature

cold water

1½ lbs. prepared fruit (rhubarb, cherries, peaches, apricots, raspberries, plums, or blackberries — in fact, anything at all!)

⅓ cup superfine sugar

FOR THE GLAZE:

1 small egg white

6 sugar cubes, crushed

FOR THE FILLING:

1 small egg yolk

2 rounded tablespoons fine semolina or cornmeal

You will also need a baking sheet, lightly greased.

Make up the pastry by sifting the flour into a large mixing bowl, then rubbing the fat into it lightly with your fingertips, lifting everything up and letting it fall back into the bowl to give it a good airing. When the mixture reaches the crumb stage, sprinkle in enough cold water to bring it together to a smooth dough that leaves the bowl absolutely clean, with no crumbs left. Give it a little light knead to bring it fully together, then place the pastry in a plastic bag and refrigerate for 30 minutes.

After that, preheat the oven to 400°F. Then roll the pastry out on a flat surface to a circle of about 14 inches. As you roll, give it quarter turns so that it ends up as round as you can make it (don't worry, though, about ragged edges: they're fine). Now carefully roll the pastry around the rolling pin and transfer it to the center of the lightly greased baking sheet.

To prevent the pastry from getting soggy because of excess juice, paint the base with egg yolk (you'll need to cover about a 10-inch circle in the center), then sprinkle the semolina or cornmeal lightly over this. The semolina is there to absorb the juices, and the egg provides a waterproof coating.

Now simply pile the prepared fruit in the center of the pastry, sprinkling it with sugar as you go. Then all you do is turn in the edges of the pastry: if any breaks, just patch it back on again — it's all meant to be ragged and interesting. Brush the pastry surface all around with the egg white, then crush the sugar

A Very Easy One-Crust Pie

cubes with a rolling pin and sprinkle over the pastry (the idea of using crushed cubes is to get a less uniform look). Now pop the pie onto the highest shelf of the oven and bake for about 35 minutes, or until the crust is golden brown. Remove from the oven and serve warm with chilled crème fraîche or ice cream.

NOTES ON ONE-CRUST FRUIT PIES
Rhubarb

Try one of the following variations: Add the grated zest of 2 oranges or 1½ teaspoons grated fresh ginger (or 1 teaspoon powdered ginger) and soft brown sugar.

Cherries

Make a hazelnut pastry by adding ⅓ cup ground hazelnuts and ¼ teaspoon powdered cinnamon to the pastry ingredients on the previous page. Use only ¼ cup sugar to sweeten the fruit.

Apricots

Use pastry as above, with 1½ pounds apricots, pitted and quartered, plus ¼ cup toasted slivered almonds.

Raspberries and Red Currants

Use pastry as above, with 1¼ pounds (5 cups) raspberries, 1 cup red currants, and ¼ cup sugar to sweeten.

Blackberries and Apples

Use 1 pound apples, 2 cups blackberries, and ¼ cup sugar to sweeten.

Plums

Use pastry as above, with 1½ pounds plums, stoned and quartered, and ¼ cup sugar to sweeten.

NOTE: 2 ounces superfine sugar equals ¼ cup.

———————— ◊ ————————

English Rhubarb Cobbler

.

SERVES 6

This is a classic English version of a fruit cobbler, but speeded up with the aid of a food processor — which makes it one of the fastest baked fruit desserts imaginable.

2 lbs. rhubarb, washed and cut into 1-inch pieces	**3 teaspoons baking powder**
½ cup superfine sugar	**1 stick ice-cold butter or margarine, cut into pieces**
grated zest of an orange	**¾ cup buttermilk or whole milk**
2 tablespoons fresh orange juice	**6 brown sugar cubes, crushed coarsely**

FOR THE TOPPING:
1¾ cups flour, sifted
½ teaspoon salt

You will also need a baking dish about 9 inches in diameter and 2½ inches deep.

Preheat the oven to 425°F.

All you do is arrange the fruit, the sugar, the grated zest of one orange, and the orange juice in the baking dish, then get on with the topping. Place the sifted flour, salt, baking powder, and butter (first cut into chunks) in a food processor. Then switch it on and give it a pulse (on/off) action several times until the mixture resembles fine breadcrumbs. Then pour in the buttermilk or whole milk and switch on again briefly until you have a thick, very sticky dough.

Now spoon tablespoons of the mixture over the fruit — the more haphazardly you do this, the better. Lastly, sprinkle the crushed sugar over the top of the dough, then pop the dish onto a high shelf in the oven for 25 to 30 minutes, or until it is a crusty golden brown. Serve it warm from the oven.

Mixed Fruit Variation

Use 2 pounds mixed fruit — peaches, apricots, plums, raspberries — with ¼ cup sugar.

—— ◊ ——

Coconut Lime Cake

·

SERVES 8

zest and juice of 2 limes
1 cup flaked coconut
1¼ cups self-rising flour
¾ cup superfine sugar
1½ sticks margarine or butter, at room temperature
3 large eggs, lightly beaten
1½ teaspoons baking powder

FOR THE ICING:
2 limes
2½ cups confectioners' sugar

You will also need 2 × 8-inch nonstick cake pans 1½ inches deep.

Preheat the oven to 325°F.

For the cake, start off by grating the zest of the 2 limes onto a small saucer, then cover with plastic wrap and set aside. Next measure the flaked coconut into a small bowl, then squeeze the juice of the limes and pour this over the coconut to allow it to soften and soak up the juice for an hour or so.

To make the cake, just take a large, roomy bowl and sift in the flour, lifting the sieve up high to give the flour a good airing. Then simply throw in all the other ingredients, including the lime zest and soaked coconut, and, with an electric hand beater switched to high speed, beat everything till thoroughly blended — about 2 to 3 minutes.

Now divide the mixture equally between the two pans, smooth to level off the tops, and bake on a middle shelf of the oven for 30 to 35 minutes, or until the centers feel springy to the touch. Allow the cake layers to cool in their pans for 5 minutes, then turn them out onto a wire rack to cool. They must be completely cooled before the icing goes on.

To make the icing, begin by removing the zest from the limes — this is best done with a zester, as you need long, thin, curly strips that look pretty. With your sharpest knife, remove all the outer pith, then carefully remove each segment (holding the limes over a bowl to catch any juice), sliding the knife in next to the membrane so that you have the flesh of the segments only. This is much easier to do with limes than it is with other citrus fruits. Drop the segments into the bowl and squeeze the last drops of juice from the pith.

Now sift the confectioners' sugar in on top of the limes a little at a time, carefully folding it in with a tablespoon in order not to break up the lime segments too much. When all the sugar is incorporated, allow the mixture to stand for 5 minutes, then spread half of it onto the surface of one of the cake layers. Place the other cake layer on top, spread the rest of the icing on top of that, and scatter the zest over. Then place the cake in the refrigerator for 30 minutes to firm up the icing before serving.

◊

Coconut Lime Cake

Pile-It-High Orange *and* Rhubarb Meringue Pie

·

SERVES 6 TO 8

T*he flavor of orange zest does something quite magical to the flavor of rhubarb, and this light, fluffy meringue pie is a perfect dessert for late spring. "Pile-it-high meringue," incidentally, applies only if you have extra egg whites to use up or* want *to make the meringue high. If not, you can simply use the 3 egg whites called for in the recipe: it will still be superb!*

FOR THE PASTRY:
¾ stick butter or margarine

1¼ cups flour

cold water to mix

FOR THE FILLING:
1½ lbs. rhubarb

grated zest and juice of 3 oranges

⅓ cup superfine sugar

3 egg yolks

3 tablespoons cornstarch

FOR THE MERINGUE:
3 large egg whites (minimum)

¾ cup superfine sugar

or

you can use as many egg whites as you have:

4 egg whites need 1 cup sugar,

5 need 1¼ cups sugar,

6 need 1½ cups sugar

You will also need a 9-inch pie pan with a high fluted edge, 1¼ inches deep, lightly greased, and a baking sheet.

Preheat the oven to 375°F, and preheat the baking sheet as well.

Begin by making the pastry: Rub the fat into the flour and add enough cold water to make a smooth dough that leaves the bowl clean. Then wrap it in a plastic bag and refrigerate for 30 minutes to let it rest. Meanwhile, wash and trim the rhubarb and cut it into chunks, place it in a shallow baking dish, and sprinkle in the grated orange zest, followed by the sugar.

Take the pastry from the refrigerator, roll it out to a round (giving it quarter turns as you do so), and use it to line the pan, pressing it up a little way above the rim. Next, prick the base all over with a fork and use some of the egg yolks to paint all over the base and sides to provide a seal. Put the pan on the preheated baking sheet on a high shelf in the oven and place the rhubarb on the lowest shelf. The pastry should take about 20 to 25 minutes to brown and crisp, and the rhubarb about 25 to 30 minutes to become soft. Then remove them from the oven.

While you're waiting for all this, you can squeeze the orange juice into a small saucepan. Use a little of it to mix the cornstarch to a smooth paste in a bowl, then bring the rest up to a simmer. Next, pour the hot orange juice onto the cornstarch mixture and pour the whole lot back into the saucepan. Beat over the heat with a small wire whisk till it becomes very thick indeed, then remove it from the heat.

Now strain the cooked rhubarb over a bowl, add the rhubarb juices and the egg yolks to the cornstarch mixture, and still beating, bring it up to a boil again. Remove from the heat, tip the strained rhubarb into the bowl, and stir it into the cornstarch mixture.

Now, for the meringue, put the egg whites into a large, clean, roomy bowl, and using an electric hand beater, beat them until they reach the stage where, when you take out the beater, little peaks stand up and just slightly turn over. Next, add the sugar, 1 tablespoon at a time, beating well after each addition. Pour the rhubarb mixture into the pastry shell, then spoon the meringue mixture over, making sure that it covers the edges of the pastry with no gaps. Then just pile it on—"normal," high, or very high. Place the pie on the center shelf of the oven, at the same temperature as before, and bake it for 25 minutes, or until the outside of the meringue is golden. Remove it from the oven and leave for about 2 hours before serving.

———————— ◊ ————————

Hazelnut Shortbread *with* Summer Fruits

·

SERVES 8

These are whisper-thin rounds of hazelnut shortcake, which make a crunchy contrast to the sharpness of summer fruits. The best way to fill them is to make a summer fruit coulis (sauce) and combine this with a mixture of whole summer fruits — and if you want to go the whole hog, some chilled heavy cream will make it sensational.

FOR THE HAZELNUT SHORTBREAD:

⅔ **cup hazelnuts**

1¼ **sticks butter, at room temperature**

½ **cup confectioners' sugar**

1 **cup sifted flour**

⅓ **cup sifted white rice flour**

FOR THE FRUIT FILLING:

1 **cup red currants**

1 **cup blueberries**

2 **tablespoons sugar**

2 **cups raspberries**

2 **cups strawberries**

FOR THE FRUIT COULIS:

1 **cup prepared red currants**

1 **cup prepared strawberries**

½ **cup prepared raspberries**

¼ **cup sugar**

confectioners' sugar for dusting

You will also need 2 large heavy baking sheets, lightly greased, and a 3½-inch round pastry cutter.

Preheat the oven to 350°F.

For the shortbread, you first need to lightly toast the hazelnuts by spreading them out on an ovenproof plate, popping them into the oven, and toasting them for 10 minutes. Then, to remove their papery skins, you rub them in a dish towel or between sheets of paper towels. Place them in a food processor and process to grind them down finely, until they look rather like coursely ground almonds.

Now in a mixing bowl cream the butter and sugar together until light and fluffy, then gradually work in the sifted flours, followed by the hazelnuts, bringing the mixture together to a stiff ball. Next, place the dough in a plastic bag and leave it in the refrigerator to rest for 30 minutes. After that, transfer it to a flat surface and roll it out to a thickness of about ¼ inch, then stamp out sixteen rounds by placing the cutter on the pastry and just giving it a sharp tap (don't twist it at all: simply lift the cutter and the piece will drop out).

Arrange the rounds on the baking sheets and lightly prick each one with a fork. Bake them for 10 to 12 minutes, or until light brown. Cool on the baking sheet for about 10 minutes, then remove to a wire rack to cool completely.

For the fruit filling, place the red currants and blueberries in a saucepan, add the sugar, then place over medium heat and let them cook for 3 to 4 minutes, or until the juice begins to run. Transfer them to a bowl, and when they're quite cold, gently stir in the raspberries and strawberries.

The coulis is made simply by soaking the fruits in the sugar for 30 minutes, then blending or processing them to make a smooth sauce and passing it through a fine sieve to extract the seeds.

Just before serving, gently fold the whole fruits into the sauce and use the mixture to sandwich the hazelnut biscuits together, then dust with confectioners' sugar before taking to the table.

———————— ◊ ————————

CHAPTER ELEVEN

SUMMER PICKLES
and
PRESERVES

◇

One of the recurring joys of summer for me is saving a little bit of it for the winter. On a gray winter day, as you spread Fresh Apricot Preserves (page 186) on your toasted English muffin, you can re-call — almost smell — that lovely basket of apricots, warm and glow-ing in the sun.

As for pickles, peaches have proved very versatile. They're great at Christmas served with ham and cold cuts, or if you warm them a little, they go particu-larly well with roast pork or duck, and for vegetarians they make an excellent accompaniment to the savory cheesecake on page 94. This year's star chutney is made with green beans: in fact I find it is the only way to preserve them, as they don't freeze at all well. So still to have a taste of them in the winter is a joy. Finally, Italian sun-dried tomatoes are rapidly becoming a regular pantry item: if you have a glut of homegrown tomatoes you may not be able to dry them in the Calabrian sunshine, but you *can* dry them in a domestic oven and store them in olive oil. The results are very good and a lot less expensive than buying them sun-dried.

Preceding pages: Spiced Pickled Green Beans (recipe on page 185)

Sweet Pickled Cucumber Slices

.

MAKES ABOUT 1½–2 QUARTS

*T*his is a marvelous pickle to serve as an accompaniment to plain grilled fish or cold cuts — or, best of all, as a snack with pâté and toast.

3 large cucumbers	**¼ teaspoon ground cloves**
3 large onions	**1 tablespoon mustard seeds**
¼ cup salt	
2½ cups white wine vinegar	**You will also need 3–4**
2½ cups soft brown sugar	**Mason-type sterilized jars**
½ teaspoon turmeric	**(1-pint size). See Note below.**

First of all, thinly slice the cucumbers, leaving the skins on, and then thinly slice the onions. Now take a large colander and layer the cucumbers and onions in it, sprinkling each layer with salt. Place a suitably sized plate over them and press it down with a heavy weight. Place the colander over a dish or bowl to catch the escaping juice and leave it like that for 3 hours. Then pour off or squeeze out as much liquid as possible.

Now put the vinegar, sugar, and spices into a large enamel or stainless-steel saucepan and stir over medium heat until the sugar has completely dissolved. Next, add the drained cucumber and onion slices, bring it all to a boil, and simmer (uncovered) for *1 minute* only. Remove the pan from the heat, and using a slotted spoon, spoon the cucumber and onion into jars. Next, boil the spiced vinegar mixture (again uncovered) for 15 minutes and then pour it into the warmed sterilized jars. Seal the jars and label when cool. Store for a month before serving.

NOTE: To prepare the jars, stand them on a rack in a large kettle, add water to cover, bring to a full rolling boil, cover kettle, and boil for 10 minutes.

◊

Preserved Pickled Peaches
(or Nectarines)

·

MAKES ABOUT 1 QUART

*W*hen there's a glut of peaches going for a song on the market, that's the time to pickle some to keep for the winter. They are lovely served with hot baked ham, roast pork, or duck. If you're a vegetarian, these peaches and the savory cheesecake on page 94 make a very good combination. The recipe works well for nectarines, too.

1½ cups granulated sugar	3 shallots, peeled and finely sliced
2½ cups white wine vinegar	
2 tablespoons fresh lime juice	
1 tablespoon coriander seeds	You will also need a 1-quart Mason-type jar, sterilized as described on page 181.
1 tablespoon mixed colored peppercorns	

Begin by measuring the sugar, wine vinegar, lime juice, coriander seeds, peppercorns, and shallots into a large enamel or stainless-steel saucepan or preserving pan. Give everything a hefty stir, then place the pan on a low heat and allow to heat through, stirring from time to time, until all the sugar has dissolved. Don't let it come up to a simmer until all the granules of sugar have completely dissolved.

While that's happening, put another saucepan of water on to boil. Then halve the peaches (by slitting them all around with a knife and twisting them in half), remove the pits, and drop the peach halves into the boiling water, a few at a time, just for a few seconds. Remove them with a slotted spoon and you should find that the skins slip off easily.

Now place the skinned peach halves in the vinegar-and-sugar mixture, bring it to a simmer, and gently poach the fruit for 15 minutes, or until tender when tested with a skewer. Use a slotted spoon to remove the peaches and transfer them to the warmed sterilized preserving jar. Now boil the syrup rapidly to reduce it to about half its original volume, then pour it through a strainer over the peaches. If you have any syrup left, reserve it, as you will find that after about 24 hours the peaches will have absorbed some of their syrup and you can use the rest to top them off. Seal the jar and keep for 6 weeks before using.

———————— ◊ ————————

Preserved Pickled Peaches

Pickled Limes

.

MAKES ENOUGH TO FILL ABOUT 3 PRESERVING JARS (½-PINT SIZE)

*T*his *is very sharp and concentrated. It goes wonderfully with fish, especially crab cakes (page 40). It is also good with the Baked Thai Red Curry Chicken on page 116 — but because it's so strong, very little is needed.*

12 to 14 fresh limes
4 tablespoons salt
½ cup water
1⅓ cups sugar
12 whole cloves
12 whole black peppercorns

You will also need a nonmetallic tray measuring about 15 × 10 inches and 3 Mason-type jars (½-pint size), sterilized as described on page 181.

You need to begin this recipe the night before, as the limes have to be salted to extract their bitterness. To do this, slice off and discard the ends of 6 of the limes, then cut into slices (skin and all) about ⅛ inch thick. Now spread a layer of paper towels all over the nonmetallic tray and lay the slices of lime on it in a single layer with no overlapping. Sprinkle half the salt over the limes, leave them like that for a few hours, then turn them over and sprinkle the rest of the salt over the other side. Cover loosely with another layer of paper towels and refrigerate overnight.

Next day, rinse the lime slices in a colander, sluicing and turning them under a cold running tap until all traces of salt have been washed away. Now transfer them to an enamel or stainless-steel saucepan with just enough water to cover them and simmer very gently for about 30 to 45 minutes, or until the slices are very tender (watch this carefully after 30 minutes are up, otherwise it's possible that they can overcook and turn to mush: the slices need to be tender but still intact).

Now squeeze the juice from the other limes — you need ¾ cup in all, and sometimes this can mean 6 limes, sometimes 7 or 8, depending on their size and juiciness. Place the juice in a saucepan, along with ½ cup water, the sugar, and the spices. Stir over a gentle heat until the sugar has dissolved completely, then simmer very gently for 25 minutes without a lid. The liquid will reduce slightly, but do keep an eye on it, as it mustn't boil rapidly or it will tend to caramelize.

Remove the syrup from the heat and take out the spices using a slotted spoon. Now add the drained lime slices to the syrup and pour the whole lot into the warmed sterilized jars. Seal them down, label when cold, and keep for a month before eating.

———————— ◊ ————————

Spiced Pickled Green Beans

.

MAKES ABOUT 2 QUARTS

T*his recipe was given to me by Kathleen Field from Bungay in Suffolk, and was first pub-lished in the* Food Aid Cookbook *in 1986. She said then, "There comes a time in late summer when the family say, 'Oh, not more runner beans again.' Well, they must be picked, and here's what to do with them." We've been doing just that with ours each year since then, and this chutney pickle is now a firm favorite. Thanks, Kathleen!*

1½ lbs. onions, chopped	1½ tablespoons turmeric
1¾ pints malt vinegar	3 cups brown granulated sugar
2 lbs. green beans (weighed after trimming and slicing)	
⅓ cup cornstarch	You will also need 4 Mason-type jars (1-pint size), sterilized as described on page 181.
1½ tablespoons mustard powder	

First of all, put the chopped onions into a large enamel or stainless-steel saucepan or preserving pan with one-third of the vinegar. Bring them to a simmer and let them simmer gently for about 20 minutes, or until the onions are soft.

Meanwhile, cook the sliced green beans in boiling salted water for 5 minutes, then strain them in a colander and add to the onions. Now in a small basin mix the cornstarch, mustard, and turmeric with a little of the remaining vinegar — enough to make a smooth paste — then add this paste to the onion mixture. Pour in the rest of the vinegar and simmer everything for 10 minutes. Next, stir in the sugar until it dissolves and continue to simmer for a further 15 minutes. Then pot the pickle in the warmed sterilized jars and seal and label when cold. Keep for at least a month before eating.

———————— ◊ ————————

Fresh Apricot Preserves

.

MAKES ABOUT 1½ QUARTS

*T**his is my mother's recipe, and every year she waits patiently for the price of apricots to come down — which usually happens in August. What she particularly likes is if, at the end of a warm summer day, whole boxes of apricots at an outdoor greenmarket are sold off at bargain prices.*

2 lbs. fresh apricots	**You will also need 3 or 4 Mason-type**
4 cups granulated sugar	**jars (1-pint size), sterilized as**
juice of 1 large lemon	**described on page 181.**
a trace of butter	

Begin this the night before you actually want to make the jam. Take a large enamel or stainless-steel saucepan or small preserving pan and grease the base with a smear of butter to prevent any sticking. Halve the apricots (reserving the pits) and place them in layers in the pan, sprinkling the sugar in between the layers. Add the lemon juice, then cover with a cloth and leave them overnight — this presoaking in sugar firms up the fruit and will ensure that the apricot pieces stay intact when you come to make the jam. At the same time, crack approximately half the apricot stones with a nutcracker and remove the kernels. Now blanch them in boiling water for 1 to 2 minutes, then drain and dry them and slip off their skins. Reserve the kernels to add to the preserve later.

To make the preserve, first pop three small plates into the refrigerator (this is for testing the set), then place the pan over a medium heat and let the sugar melt and completely dissolve — about 15 minutes. The sugar must be absolutely clear and free of granules, otherwise the preserve will be sugary. When the sugar has dissolved, turn the heat up to its very highest and let the mixture boil rapidly for about 10 to 20 minutes, stirring from time to time to prevent sticking.

Next, use the cold plates to test for a set. Remove the pan from the heat and place a teaspoonful of the preserve on one of the plates. Allow it to cool for a few seconds, then push it with your finger: if a crinkly skin has formed on the jam, then it has set. If it hasn't set, boil it again for another 5 minutes and do another test. When you have a set, remove the mixture from the heat and stir in a trace of butter, which will disperse any scum that has formed. Then add the reserved kernels and let the preserves settle for 15 minutes before pouring them into warmed sterilized jars. Seal while still warm and label the jars when cool.

———————— ◊ ————————

Fresh Apricot Preserves

Preserved Dried Tomatoes

·

MAKES ABOUT 1 QUART

If you grow your own tomatoes, or can get hold of a good quantity when they're going cheap, it really is worth preserving them for use in the winter. Although they're not dried in the Italian sunshine like the imported kind, I have found that the oven-dried variety still have a lovely concentrated flavor.

6 lbs. ripe but firm medium-sized tomatoes
3 teaspoons salt
2½ cups extra-virgin olive oil
4 basil leaves

You will also need 4 Mason-type jars (½-pint size), sterilized as described on page 181, and 2 wire racks.

Preheat the oven to 175°F.

Begin by washing the tomatoes and removing the stems, then slice them in half across the middle, turn the cut sides down on a plate, and squeeze out the seeds. Lay some double layers of kitchen towels on a work surface and leave each half upside down on them to drain while you get on with preparing the rest.

When they're all ready, turn them over and very lightly sprinkle the insides with salt — don't overdo this or you will lose the lovely concentrated sweetness the tomatoes should have when they are dried. Now lay the tomatoes, cut side down, on the wire racks, leaving just enough space between them so that they do not touch. Next, lay some foil on the bottom shelf of the oven to catch any drips and save on oven cleaning, then place the two racks in the oven, leaving space for the air to circulate freely between the shelves.

As you close the door, wedge it with a skewer (or something similar) to stop it from closing completely — it needs only about a ¼-inch gap, just sufficient to stop the buildup of heat so that the tomatoes dry rather than cook.

If the tomatoes are of medium size, they will probably need 8 hours to dry completely, but take a look at them after 6 hours and remove any that appear to be ready. At this stage, you can turn them the other way up. What you want is for the tomatoes to be dried but still retain a slight fleshy feel — don't let them go too papery. If in doubt, taste one: they should be chewy and have a concentrated sweet tomato flavor.

When the tomatoes are cool, pack them into the warmed sterilized jars — not too tightly — and top up with the oil and a basil leaf in each one before sealing and labeling.

NOTE: I have stored these for 6 months and they have kept beautifully.

———————————— ◊ ————————————

CHAPTER TWELVE

BREAD, PIZZA, *and* FOCACCIA

———— ◇ ————

Summer, when the weather is hot and energy levels are low, is perhaps not the best time to be baking bread. The last thing I feel like doing is kneading dough in a hot kitchen on a sunny day. However, even during the summer, the truth is that there is always a fair (or unfair!) proportion of rainy days — and that's when a spot of bread making can be very therapeutic and comforting.

There's another good reason for making the breads in this chapter: All of them have a variety of ingredients and flavors, and while we're all struggling to do without butter, it makes life much more interesting if the bread itself has its own individuality and interest to compensate for the lack of butter. So find a cloudy day and bake a batch of flavored breads for the freezer.

NOTES ON BREAD MAKING
Active Dry Yeast

Yeast is what enables bread to rise, and active dry yeast has more or less superseded the fresh and other dried varieties. All you do with this is sprinkle the required amount in with the flour and then add the water. Each pound of flour needs a ¼-ounce package of yeast. But a warning: do inspect the date stamp carefully, as fast-rising, active dry yeast will not do its work once it becomes stale.

Kneading

Where kneading is necessary, simply place the dough on a flat work surface and stretch it away from you, using the heel of one hand to push from the middle and the clenched knuckles of your other hand to pull the other half of the dough toward you — both hands should move simultaneously to stretch out the dough. Then lift the edges over and back to the middle. Give it a quarter turn and repeat the process. It soon becomes a rather rhythmic operation, and the dough will then start to become very elastic. This is the gluten at work. In simple terms the water meets the gluten and what makes it become springy and alive is a good pummeling. A properly kneaded piece of dough will look plump and rounded, with a very smooth surface.

Rising

The dough must be left to rise for a specified period to allow the yeast to do its work: all yeast doughs need at least an hour at room temperature before baking, or less in a warm draft-free place, which does speed up the rising. But care should be taken not to place it too near to direct heat, as too high a temperature can kill off the yeast. Always cover the dough, either with a folded damp dish towel or with plastic wrap. When properly risen, the dough should have doubled in size and should spring back and feel very slightly sticky when lightly touched with the finger. Remember that the longer the rising time, the more uniformly the yeast will work and the more evenly textured the finished bread will be.

Punching Down and Proving

Some recipes call for a second rising or "proving," which is exactly what it is: the yeast proving that it is still alive and active. The proving ensures there will be an even rise. Punching down is simply punching all the gas out of the dough and bringing it back to its original size to allow it to rise for a second time.

Baking

Loaf pans should always be greased generously. I use butter for this and spread it evenly around with a piece of waxed paper. Always bake bread in a hot oven, and bear in mind it's always better to overcook rather than undercook bread. To test if a loaf is cooked, tap it on the underside with your knuckles, and if it sounds hollow, it's done. If you like very crusty bread, after you've turned the loaves out of their pans, pop them back in the oven upside down for 5 to 10 minutes.

Cooling

Always cool bread on a wire rack. If you place it directly on a flat surface, the steam will be trapped and you'll find that the crust will become soggy. Also, a loaf that has not been properly cooled before freezing or storing can taste doughy.

Mini-Focaccia Bread *with* Four Toppings

·

MAKES 1 LARGE FOCACCIA OR 4 MINI-FOCACCIAS

*F*ocaccia is an Italian flat bread made with olive oil. The flavor of the oil is important, so it's advisable to use a good, strong, fruity virgin olive oil for this. What's good about focaccia is that it gives you scope to invent all kinds of interesting toppings. Below I've given the basic recipe for making either one full-size focaccia or four mini ones. You can also vary the toppings — that is, if you cut the topping ingredients down to a quarter of the original quantity, you can have four minis with a different topping on each one (as in the photograph opposite).

FOR THE BASIC FOCACCIA DOUGH:	1½ teaspoons active dry yeast
2½ cups white bread flour	1 cup warm water
½ teaspoon salt	1½ tablespoons extra-virgin olive oil

Begin by sifting the flour and salt into a large bowl, then sprinkle in the yeast and mix that in. Next, pour in the warm water along with the olive oil and mix everything to a dough that leaves the sides of the bowl clean (if necessary you can add a few more drops of water). Now turn the dough out onto a lightly floured surface and knead it for about 10 minutes. (Alternatively, you can use an electric mixer with a dough hook and process for 5 minutes.)

When the dough feels very bouncy and elastic, return it to the bowl, cover with plastic wrap, and leave in a warm place until it has doubled in size (about 1½ hours or more, depending on the heat in the kitchen. If there's no suitable warm place, you can sit the bowl over a saucepan of warm water, but not over direct heat). After that, turn the dough out onto the work surface and punch the air out by kneading it again for 2 to 3 minutes. Now it's ready for a topping.

If you're making a full-sized focaccia, pat the dough out into an approximate oval shape 12 × 10 inches, arrange your chosen topping over (or into) the whole thing, and proceed as described on page 196, except that the large focaccia will take 25 to 30 minutes to cook.

————————— ◊ —————————

Clockwise from the top: Mini-Focaccia Bread with Coarse-Salt Topping; Blue Cheese, Garlic, and Thyme Topping; Red Onion, Olive, and Rosemary Topping; Basil and Sun-Dried Tomato Topping (pages 196–98)

Red Onion, Olive, *and* Rosemary Topping

.

MAKES ENOUGH FOR 4 MINI-FOCACCIAS OR 1 LARGE FOCACCIA

1⅓ cups pitted black olives, halved	1 teaspoon coarse salt
4 teaspoons chopped fresh rosemary	1 tablespoon olive oil
2 small red onions, halved and then sliced into ¼-inch wedges	

Take two-thirds of the olives and push them evenly into the dough, then divide the dough into four and place the sections on an oiled baking sheet, using your hands to pat out each piece into an oblong shape, rounded at the ends and measuring 4 × 3 inches. Next, sprinkle a quarter of the remaining olives and a quarter of the rosemary and onions onto each piece. Finally, sprinkle the surface with salt and drizzle the olive oil all over each focaccia. Cover with a damp dish towel and leave the dough to puff up again for 30 minutes.

Meanwhile, preheat the oven to 375°F. When the 30 minutes are up, bake the breads in the oven for about 15 minutes or until they are golden around the edges and look well cooked in the center. Cool on a wire rack and serve warm.

———————— ◊ ————————

Coarse-Salt Topping

.

MAKES ENOUGH FOR 4 MINI-FOCACCIAS OR 1 LARGE FOCACCIA

1 tablespoon olive oil	4 teaspoons coarse salt

If you are making the 4 mini-focaccias, divide the dough into four, put the pieces on an oiled baking sheet, and pull and push each one into shape as described above. Then drizzle the olive oil over the surface of each one and sprinkle the coarse salt over them. Cover with a damp dish towel and leave for 30 minutes for the dough to puff up. Meanwhile, preheat the oven to 375°F and bake the focaccias for about 15 minutes. Cool on a wire rack and serve warm.

———————— ◊ ————————

Blue Cheese, Garlic, *and* Thyme Topping

.

MAKES ENOUGH FOR 4 MINI-FOCACCIAS OR 1 LARGE FOCACCIA

4 teaspoons fresh thyme leaves	**4 large cloves garlic, cut lengthwise**
freshly ground black pepper	**into thin matchstick strips**
6 ozs. gorgonzola cheese	**1 tablespoon olive oil**

Divide the dough into four, place the pieces on an oiled baking sheet, and pull and push each one into shape as described on page 196. Then cover the surface of each one with the thyme leaves and a fairly liberal grinding of black pepper. Next, remove the rind from the gorgonzola and dice the cheese. Sprinkle over the surface of the four pieces of dough, together with the strips of garlic. Now drizzle the olive oil over the surface of the toppings, cover with a damp dish towel, and leave to puff up again for 30 minutes. Meanwhile, preheat the oven to 375°F and bake the focaccias for about 15 minutes. Cool on a wire rack and serve warm.

———————— ◊ ————————

Basil *and* Sun-Dried Tomato Topping

MAKES ENOUGH FOR 4 MINI-FOCACCIAS OR 1 LARGE FOCACCIA

about 24 fresh basil leaves	1 teaspoon coarse salt
2 ozs. sun-dried tomatoes preserved in oil, drained and chopped small	1 tablespoon olive oil

Take 12 of the basil leaves and tear them into small pieces, then push them evenly into the dough. Divide the dough into four pieces, place them on an oiled baking sheet, and pull and push them into shape (as described on page 196). Gently push the sun-dried tomatoes into the surface of each piece of dough. Next, sprinkle the remaining basil leaves onto the dough along with the salt, and finally drizzle the olive oil over the surface of the topping. Cover with a damp dish towel and leave for 30 minutes for the dough to puff up. Meanwhile preheat the oven to 375°F, and bake the focaccias for about 15 minutes. Cool on a wire rack and serve warm.

◊

Sun-Dried Tomato *and* Ricotta Bread

·

MAKES 12 ROLLS OR 30 BREADSTICKS

T*his is a lovely, moist bread, which I like to make into individual rolls or breadsticks. The latter are great to munch on at a supper party while everyone is waiting for the first course.*

1 cup multigrain flour	**1½ tablespoons chopped fresh basil leaves**
1½ cups white bread flour	
1 tablespoon steel-cut oats	**¾ cup warm water**
1½ teaspoons active dry yeast	**4 ozs. ricotta cheese, at room temperature**
1 teaspoon salt	
1 oz. sun-dried tomatoes preserved in oil, drained and chopped small	**2 tablespoons olive oil (from the tomatoes, if possible)**

First, take a large, roomy bowl and sift the flours into it. Now sprinkle in the oats, yeast, salt, tomatoes, and basil and mix well. After that, make a well in the center of the mixture, pour the water onto the flour, and begin to mix it a little. Then add the cheese and olive oil and keep mixing till you have a smooth dough.

Now knead the dough for 5 minutes, or until it becomes springy and elastic (this can be done in a mixer or a food processor with a dough-kneading attachment). After that, cover the bowl with plastic wrap and leave the dough to prove till doubled in size — I can't give a timing on this because it depends on the kitchen temperature, but don't hurry it, as the bread will be better if it has a longer proving time.

When it has doubled in size, remove the dough from the bowl onto a lightly floured surface and punch it down to release all the air. Now you can shape it either into twelve rolls, knots, cottage shapes, or plain rounds, or into breadsticks. To make breadsticks, roll into 30 fat pencil shapes, then slash diagonally with a knife. Arrange the rolls on separate greased baking sheets, cover with plastic wrap, and leave to rise once more to double in size.

Meanwhile, preheat the oven to 425°F. Bake the rolls for 18 to 20 minutes, or the breadsticks for 10 to 12 minutes. Cool on a wire rack. These will freeze well in sealed freezer bags.

◊

Green Peppercorn Bread

·

MAKES 15 ROLLS OR 50 BREADSTICKS

This is a lovely, gutsy, spicy bread.

3⅓ cups white bread flour	1 tablespoon dried green peppercorns, crushed in a mortar with a pestle
1 package (¼ oz.) active dry yeast	3 tablespoons extra-virgin olive oil
2 teaspoons salt	
1¼ cups warm water	**You will also need 2 heavy baking sheets.**

Begin by sifting the flour into a large bowl, then sprinkle in the yeast and the salt, make a well in the center and pour in the warm water. Begin to mix a little, then add the crushed peppercorns and olive oil and continue mixing until you have a smooth dough. Now knead the dough for 5 minutes, or until it becomes springy and elastic, and after that cover the bowl with plastic wrap and leave it to prove till doubled in size — the length of time will depend on the kitchen temperature, but at all events don't rush it, because the longer the proving time, the better the bread.

When it has doubled in size, remove the dough from the bowl to a lightly floured surface, then punch it down to release the air. Now you can shape it either into rolls or breadsticks, in which case roll out the dough into 50 fat pencil shapes, slashed diagonally with a knife. Arrange them on separate greased baking sheets, cover with plastic wrap, and leave to rise once more to double in size.

Meanwhile preheat the oven to 425°F. Bake the rolls for 18 to 20 minutes, or the breadsticks for 10 to 12 minutes. Cool on a wire rack. Both freeze successfully in sealed freezer bags.

————————— ◊ —————————

Whole-Grain Bread *with* Sunflower *and* Poppy Seeds

·

MAKES 2 LOAVES (1 POUND EACH)

I love the flavor and nutty texture of this loaf, which, when it's a couple of days old, toasts really well — lovely with some homemade preserves for breakfast and so good there's no need for butter!

3⅓ cups whole-wheat flour	1½ cups warm water
2 teaspoons salt	2 tablespoons olive oil
1 package (¼ oz.) active dry yeast	
¾ cup sunflower seeds	**You will also need 2 loaf pans**
3 tablespoons poppy seeds	**8½ × 4½ × 2½ inches, well buttered.**
1 tablespoon soft dark brown sugar	

First of all, sift the flour and salt together in a large bowl, then sprinkle in the yeast and give a good stir to mix it in. Next add the sunflower and poppy seeds and mix again. Now dissolve the sugar in the water, pour this over the flour, together with the oil, and mix everything to a dough. Knead it well for 5 minutes, then cover the bowl with plastic wrap and leave it to rise until doubled in size.

When it has doubled its bulk, turn the dough out onto a lightly floured surface and knead it once again. Now divide the dough into two, pull each piece into a length, fold one edge to the center and the other on top of that, and then place the loaves in the greased pans. Cover and leave to prove again, and meanwhile preheat the oven to 400°F.

When the dough has risen to the top of the pans, place them in the oven on a highish shelf and bake for 40 minutes. Turn the loaves out and return them without pans, upside down, to the oven (to crisp the edges) for a further 5 minutes. Then cool on a wire rack.

—————— ◊ ——————

Skillet Pizza *with* Smoked Mozzarella *and* Sun-Dried Tomatoes

SERVES 2 AS A MAIN COURSE OR 4 AS A FIRST COURSE

*T*his is the easiest homemade pizza in the world. It's made with a scone dough, which happily does not require kneading and proving. The topping can, of course, be varied to include whatever you like best, but the combination below is, I think, one of the nicest. If you don't have time to make up the tomato sauce, you can substitute ¼ cup of tomato paste.

FOR THE TOMATO SAUCE:

1 tablespoon olive oil

1 small onion, chopped

1 medium clove garlic, crushed

1 lb. tomatoes, skinned and chopped

1 tablespoon chopped fresh basil

salt and freshly ground black pepper

FOR THE BASE:

1½ cups self-rising flour

½ teaspoon salt

freshly ground black pepper

1 tablespoon chopped fresh herbs

¼ cup olive oil

water

FOR THE TOPPING:

5 ozs. smoked mozzarella, cut into ½-inch pieces

4 ozs. sun-dried tomatoes preserved in oil, drained and chopped

12 black olives, pitted and sliced

2 ozs. mushrooms, sliced

2 tablespoons capers, drained

2 tablespoons torn fresh basil leaves

salt and freshly ground black pepper

2 tablespoons preserved tomato oil (from the sun-dried tomatoes, above)

First, make up the tomato sauce by heating the olive oil in a small saucepan, adding the onion and garlic, and cooking for 2 to 3 minutes to soften. Then add the chopped tomatoes and basil, season with salt and pepper, and continue to cook over medium heat for 20 to 25 minutes, until the tomatoes have reduced and concentrated their flavor. (While you're at it, why not make a larger quantity of this — it freezes very well!)

Now for the pizza base: Sift the flour into a bowl along with some seasoning and the herbs. Make a well in the center and pour in 2 tablespoons of the olive oil, followed by 4 tablespoons of water. Mix to a soft (though not sticky) dough — you may find that you have to add a further tablespoon or so of water to get the right consistency.

Next, prepare a floured surface, turn the dough out onto it, and knead lightly before rolling out to a round to fit the base of a 9- to 10-inch skillet. Heat 1 tablespoon of the remaining olive oil in the pan, place the circle of dough in it, and cook over a low heat for about 5 minutes, or until the base is lightly browned. Have ready an oiled plate and turn the pizza base out onto it. Then, after heating the last remaining tablespoon of olive oil in the pan, slide the pizza back in and cook the reverse side for 5 minutes.

During this time, spread the reduced tomato sauce over the surface of the pizza, then scatter the pieces of mozzarella, the dried tomatoes, the olives, the mushrooms, the capers, and the torn basil leaves over the tomato sauce. Season, then drizzle the oil from the preserved tomatoes over the top. To see if the underside of the pizza is cooked, you can lift up a corner with a spatula and have a look. When it's ready, transfer the pan to a preheated broiler for 2 to 3 minutes to melt the cheese and heat the topping. Serve straightaway.

◇

Summer Entertaining

Below are a few suggested menus for a variety of summer entertaining.

A SUPPER PARTY FOR 8 PEOPLE

First Course
Mixed-Leaf Caesar Salad* (page 20)

Sun-Dried Tomato and Ricotta
Bread rolls (page 199)

Main Course
Baked Lamb with Rosemary with
Red Currant and Mint Sauce
(page 110)

Sliced Potatoes Baked with Tomatoes
and Basil† (page 65)

Fresh shelled peas

Dessert
Cheesecake with Strawberry
Sauce (page 161)

———————— ◊ ————————

A VEGETARIAN SUPPER PARTY FOR 4 PEOPLE

First Course
Chilled Lemongrass and Cilantro
Vichyssoise (page 10)

Mini-Focaccias (page 194)

Main Course
Roasted Vegetable Couscous Salad
with Harissa-Style Dressing
(page 98)

Dessert
Vanilla Cream Terrine with
Raspberry Coulis
(page 132)

———————— ◊ ————————

A Fourth of July Barbecue for 8 People

First Course
Salad of Romaine lettuce and arugula
with Blue Cheese Dressing* (page 34)
and Olive Croutons (page 7)

Main Course
All-American Half-Pounders*
(page 78)

Mexican Tomato Salsa* (page 79)

Oven-Roasted Potatoes with Garlic
and Rosemary* (page 70)

Grilled Corn (page 83)

Dessert
Hot Fudge Sundaes* (page 147)

———————— ◊ ————————

A Quick and Easy Supper for 4 Busy People

First Course
Fresh Asparagus with Foaming
Hollandaise (page 13)

Main Course
Chicken Basque (page 120)

Mixed-leaf salad with Balsamic
Vinaigrette Dressing (page 35)

Dessert
Summer Fruit Compote (page 130)
with crème fraîche

———————— ◊ ————————

A Summer Buffet Party for 18 People
(including vegetarian choices)

First Course
Roasted Tomato Salad* (page 25)

Hot and Sour Pickled Shrimp*
(page 48)

Compote of Garlic and Sweet Bell
Peppers (page 67)

Main Course
Salmon Steaks with Avocado and
Crème Fraîche Sauce (page 46)

Oven-Baked Chicken with Garlic and
Parmigiano (page 86)

Savory Feta Cheesecake (page 94)
with Preserved Pickled Peaches
(page 182)

Pesto Rice Salad‡ (page 28)

Roasted Fennel Niçoise‡ (page 66)

Baby Summer Vegetables with Lemon
Vinaigrette‡ (page 68)

Green Peppercorn rolls† (page 200)

Whole-Grain Bread with Sunflower
and Poppy Seeds† (page 201)

Dessert
A Terrine of Summer Fruits (page 129)*

Caramel Meringues (page 162) with
Mascarpone Cream* (page 136)

Fresh Peaches Baked in Marsala with
Mascarpone Cream (page 136)

———————— ◊ ————————

*Double the recipe.
†Multiply the recipe by 1½.
‡Triple the recipe.

INDEX

◇

Page numbers in *italics* refer to illustrations.